Surviving Bomber Aircraft
of World War Two

Surviving Bomber Aircraft
of World War Two

A Global Guide to Location and Types

Don Berliner

Pen & Sword
AVIATION

First published in Great Britain in 2012 by
Pen & Sword Aviation
An imprint of
Pen & Sword Books Ltd
47 Church Street
Barnsley
South Yorkshire
S70 2AS

Copyright © Don Berliner 2012

ISBN 978 1 84884 545 9

A CIP catalogue record for this book is
available from the British Library

Typeset in 10.5pt Palatino by Mac Style, Beverley, East Yorkshire
Printed and bound in India by Replika Press Pvt. Ltd.

Pen & Sword Books Ltd incorporates the Imprints of Pen & Sword Aviation, Pen & Sword
Family History, Pen & Sword Maritime, Pen & Sword Military, Pen & Sword Discovery,
Wharncliffe Local History, Wharncliffe True Crime, Wharncliffe Transport, Pen & Sword Select,
Pen & Sword Military Classics, Leo Cooper, The Praetorian Press, Remember When,
Seaforth Publishing and Frontline Publishing

For a complete list of Pen & Sword titles please contact
PEN & SWORD BOOKS LIMITED
47 Church Street, Barnsley, South Yorkshire, S70 2AS, England
E-mail: enquiries@pen-and-sword.co.uk
Website: www.pen-and-sword.co.uk

Contents

Introduction

Combat aviation in World War Two was really about bombers.

Fighters were unquestionably the glamour airplanes. The Spitfires and Messerschmitts and Mustangs were the fastest and the most maneuverable, and their pilots were the modern counterparts of daring, flamboyant cavalrymen. But fighters were used primarily to destroy enemy bombers before they could accomplish their destructive missions, and to prevent enemy fighters from destroying their own air force's bombers.

As the war progressed, fighters became fighter-bombers, taking on some of the characteristics of bombers, with shackles under their wings that could carry hundreds and then thousands of pounds of bombs. In order to make this work, the fighter pilot had to accept the role of bombardier, in addition to the those of navigator, radioman and gunner, for which he might not have been so thoroughly trained.

Vital as they were, all other types of aircraft had to take a back seat to the bombers. Trainers existed to prepare pilots and aircrew for their primary missions. Transports delivered men and materiel to where they were needed. Reconnaissance airplanes found the targets for the bombers and the fighter-bombers, and then brought back enough information to enable analysts to determine the effectiveness of the bombing missions.

Most major air forces included the same broad sub-categories of bombers: attack, light, medium and patrol. But only the Royal Air Force and US Army Air Forces saw the need for thousands of four-engined heavy and very heavy bombers. They took the war directly to the enemy's homes and factories, and it was the lack of such long-range deliverers of bombs in the Luftwaffe that constituted one of the major, history-changing blunders on the part of the leaders of the Third Reich.

While much of the pre-war thinking about air warfare pointed to such bombers being unstoppable, the initial inability to provide them with fighter protection revealed the serious susceptibility of even the most heavily-gunned bombers to an organized attack by a swarm of enemy interceptors. It wasn't until the development of the long-range single-seat fighter capable of accompanying bombers on their longest missions, did it become feasible to send great formations deep into enemy territory in broad daylight.

In the final accounting, it was the bombers' ability to significantly interfere with the production of equipment and vital parts, such as ball bearings, that so reduced the war-making potential of both Germany and Japan, thus shortening the war and saving many thousands of lives.

Inevitably, there are a few bombers whose exact categorization has been impossible to ascertain. Is a 'reconnaissance bomber' a reconnaissance airplane or a bomber? What of a bomber that was withdrawn from combat during the war and used for training bomber pilots?

As was the case with fighters in Volume I, the World War Two types display an amazing range of technology. There was progress in just a few years from those with open cockpits, fixed landing gears and piston engines of a few hundred horsepower, to the Arado Ar.234 Blitz with four jet engines, and the Fieseler Fi 103 'buzz bomb', which lacked a human pilot.

Chapter 1

United States of America

US Army Air Corps and US Army Air Forces

Martin B-10

When the B-10's immediate predecessor, the privately financed Martin Model 123, first flew in 1932 at the factory near Baltimore, Maryland, it was not merely the fastest bomber in the world, but faster than most fighters. As such, it had little need for defensive armament, at least until the results of suddenly rapid progress in airframe design enabled it to be passed by. For a while, however, it was a completely new way of doing an old job.

It was America's first all-metal bomber that combined retractable landing gear and a fully internal bomb load into an unusually streamlined package. Almost everything that could be hidden inside where it would not produce aerodynamic drag, was safely tucked away. Suddenly, it was the picture of the future. It was what every manufacturer should have been building.

The Model 123 arrived at Wright Field in March, 1932, and was soon clocked at 197mph, thanks to a pair of 600hp Wright SR-1820 Cyclone radial engines. It was then returned to Martin for some changes. The nose gunner, who had been sitting out in the open air, was given a manually-rotated turret, though the pilot and top gunner retained their traditional canopy-less seats where the

former could feel the air on his face, long considered vital to good piloting.

Later, 675hp Wright Cyclones were installed, along with a longer, 70ft 7in wing. Top speed jumped to 207mph, increasing its advantage over then-operational fighters and bombers. For

this, the Glenn L Martin Co. was awarded the prestigious Collier Trophy. In January, 1933, the US Army bought the prototype, which it designated the XB-10, and ordered 48 production versions of the improved Model 139.

The first production airplanes were designated Y1B-10 and featured full canopies over the pilot and top gunner, and a total defensive armament of three .30 cal. machine guns, which was comparable to that of many pursuit planes of the day. Bomb load was limited to 2,200lb internally, or a single 2,000lb bomb attached to an underwing shackle. Most of the YB-10 service test airplanes were assigned to March Field, California, in late 1933, from whence they departed on a 10,000-mile proving flight to Alaska. Such demonstrations were common to that era, and were seen as highly effective public showing of a country's offensive power, and of course the need for Congressional appropriations to build fleets of planes.

The YB-10A, one of the first built, was modified with experimentally turbocharged Wright Cyclone engines. They boosted the top speed to 236mph at 25,000ft, which might well have led to a production version had the superchargers been more fully developed and reliable.

The main production version, with more than 100 ordered, was the B-10B, which differed in only minor ways from the YB-10. Its top speed was said to be 212mph, though a long-retired B-10 pilot told the author that his sole attempt to hit 200mph ended when the airplane began to shake violently at 180mph and he decided to end the unauthorized test while all the parts were still in place.

Starting in late 1935, B-10Bs were assigned to squadrons on the Atlantic and Pacific coasts, as well as the Panama Canal Zone and the Philippines. They remained in Army Air Corps service until replaced by B-17s and B-18s just prior to America's entry into the war. Only one of them saw combat. But others were built as

Martin's export business flourished. The factory Model 139W won an Argentine Air Force competition, defeating the German Junkers Ju 86 and the Italian Savoia Marchetti S.M.79, and producing an order for 39 airplanes.

Other orders came from China (for 6) which first put the airplane into action when the Japanese invaded in 1937. Another six were sold to Siam, one to the USSR, along with an order from the Dutch Indies for more than 100, of which most were to be powered by 900hp Wright Cyclones. Many of these went into action when the Japanese invaded, but most of the obsolete Martins were wiped out in the air or on the ground before they could have any great impact on the fighting.

Two further developments of the basic B-10 were the B-12A and the XB-14. The former was the last 32 of the original order for B-10Bs, powered by 775hp Pratt & Whitney R-1690 Hornet radial engines and with an internal auxiliary fuel tank to extend its combat range to 1,240 miles. The sole XB-14 had a pair of 950hp Pratt & Whitney R-1820 engines. A YB-13 was planned as a modified YB-10, but was never built. The next bomber to emerge from the Martin plant was the sleek, high-performance B-26 Marauder, the fascinating six-engined, Allison V-12-powered Martin XB-16 having never left the drawing board.

Only a single Argentine Model 139 survived to be returned to the USA in 1976. It was restored as a B-10B and has long been on public display.

Specifications of the B-10B

Length: 44ft 9in
Wingspan: 70ft 5in
Height: 15ft 6in

Wing area: 678 sq ft
Empty weight: 9,700lb
Maximum speed: 213mph
Maximum range: 1,240 miles
Service ceiling: 24,200ft
Maximum bomb load: 2,200lb

Sole Surviving Example

National Museum of the US Air Force

Boeing B-17 Flying Fortress

It was easily the best-known American bomber of the war, more than 12,000 of them having been built by Boeing, as well as by Douglas and Vega (later merged with Lockheed). It also best represented the philosophy of day bombing, in which heavy defensive armament (13 .50 cal. machine guns in the final major version, the B-17G) were expected to enable them to beat off enemy attacks so they could complete their daylight bombing raids, especially when they were flying in close formation.

When the prototype of the Model 299 (B-17) was rolled out on 27 July 1935, the Army Air Corps' first-line bomber was the Martin B-10. By comparison, the B-17's loaded weight was more than four times as great, its maximum bomb load was five times as great, and its maximum range was considerably more. It was clearly a completely new concept in bombers, and the privately funded prototype involved a major financial risk to Boeing.

In fact, the manufacturer was jumping head-first into the development of very large airplanes, including the giant B-15 one-of-a-kind very heavy bomber and the majestic Model 314 four-

engined oceanic flying boat. It was a risk Boeing would repeat many years later, and with great success, with the 747, the world's first jumbo jet airliner.

The 299's life was brief, ending in October 1935 when it crashed shortly after take-off as a result of the rudder and elevator gust locks not having been de-activated. But the Army was so impressed by the design's advanced ideas and the performance it displayed on its few test flights, that while the plan to order 65 airplanes was dropped, it was quickly replaced by a more conservative order for 13 YB-17s for realistic service tests.

As the 2nd Bombardment Group at Langley Field, Virginia, they pioneered long-range bombing tactics, including a six-plane formation making a one-stop, 5,000-mile flight from Miami to Buenos Aires, Argentina.

Opposition came from not only the US Navy, which understandably saw long-range bombers as a threat to the country's need for its carrier-based light bombers, but even from influential elements in the Army that felt the B-17's role could be filled by a larger number of twin-engined aircraft. However, the inevitable ascendancy of the long-range bomber began with the Munich Crisis in 1938 and the accelerating approach of a second world war.

Production of Flying Fortresses was slow to gain speed, with small numbers of B-17C and B-17D 'small tail' Forts being assigned to combat squadrons, the latter equipping a unit in the Philippines. Twenty B-17Cs were shipped to England, where the RAF called them Fortress I and were the first to use the type in combat, starting in July 1941.

The first of the primary versions – the B-17E with its distinctive and much larger vertical tail and dorsal fin – was ordered into quantity several months before the Japanese attack on Pearl

Harbor. It had improved defensive armament, in particular a tail turret with two .50 cal. machine guns. Only about 500 B-17Es were built, as Boeing's production capacity was being rapidly allocated to the forthcoming B-17F, which Boeing would build in Seattle and Wichita, Kansas; Douglas in Santa Monica and Long Beach, California, and Vega (soon to be absorbed by Lockheed) would together build 3,400 bombers.

Large numbers of B-17Es quickly found their way to US Army Air Forces squadrons in North Africa and the South Pacific, while a fast growing supply of them were based in England and enabled the 8th Air Force to handle the massed daylight raids on Germany and occupied countries, while the RAF did the same at night. The impact of the big bombers was being felt by all the Axis powers.

The final operational version was also the most widely produced: almost 8,700 B-17Gs were built, and can be recognized by the two-gun 'chin' turret which eliminated the last remaining major defensive blind spot.

Experimental versions of the Fortress included the B-38, with its four liquid-cooled, 1,475hp Allison V-1710 V-12 engines which boosted the top speed substantially. The engines turned out not to be available in quantity as the entire production capacity was reserved for P-38 Lightnings, P-40 Tomahawks and Bell P-39s and P-63s. In addition, there was the XB-40 with additional guns intended to allow it to serve as a bomber escort. The prototype was wrecked just a few weeks after its first flight, and soon the prospect of drop-tank-equipped long-range escort fighters such as the P-51D made it unnecessary.

The total production of all models of the B-17 reached 12,726 by the time the last one rolled off the assembly line in May 1945. It had already been replaced by the ultra-modern, sophisticated B-29 Superfortress.

The D-model 'Swoose' is the oldest B-17 that survives, having flown on the first American combat mission of the war and then on the first night bombing mission and remained in service throughout the war. After suffering extensive combat damage, it was retired in 1942 to finish its career as the personal transport of a general. In 1948, ownership was transferred to the National Air Museum (later the National Air & Space Museum), which stored it until 2008 when it was turned over to the National Museum of the US Air Force, which has long-term plans for its restoration. Its unusual name comes from a 1940s popular song having something to do with being half-swan, half-goose. And since this B-17D spent most of its days flying with the tail grafted from another model of B-17, this seemed appropriate.

Specifications of the B-17G

Length: 74ft 4in
Wingspan: 103ft 9.5in
Height: 19ft 1in
Wing area: 1,420 sq ft
Empty weight: 32,720lb
Top speed: 300mph
Range: 1,850 miles with 4,000lb bomb load
Service ceiling: 35,000ft
Maximum bomb load: 17,600lb

Some Surviving Examples

B-17D
USAAC 40-3097 52 'Swoose' – US National Air & Space Museum (at the National Museum of The US Air Force)

B-17F
USAAF 41-24485 'Memphis Belle' – Memphis, Tennessee
USAAF 44-83735 – Imperial War Museum, Duxford

B-17G
USAAF 44-83624 – National Museum of the US Air Force
USAAF 44-83684 – Planes of Fame
USAAF 44-83735 'Mary Alice' – American Air Museum at Duxford
USAAF 44-83868 – Royal Air Force Museum, Hendon
USAAF 44-85718 'Thunderbird' – Lone Star Flight Museum
USAAF 44-85784 'Sally B' – Imperial War Museum, Duxford
USAAF 44-85828 – Pima Air and Space Museum

Douglas B-18 Bolo

Douglas Aircraft Co. had never produced a bomber for the US Army, and in fact was on the verge of becoming a major force in the emerging airliner industry. Its DC-2 would soon receive a 'wide body' and become the DC-3, perhaps the most important airplane in airline history, as it made profitable operations possible without government subsidy.

Then someone got the idea that, with suitable changes, the basic DC-2 could become a long-range bomber, and thus the B-18 Bolo was born. A 1934 Army competition for a long-range bomber required entrants to design a bomber that would carry 2,000lb of bombs for 2,000 miles at 200mph. Martin entered an improved B-10, Boeing created its Model 299 which would become the immortal B-17 and Douglas offered its B-18. The Martin design had little chance, and the Boeing prototype crashed before completing the main tests of the competition, leaving the B-18 as the winner.

The DC-2 received a new, deeper fuselage that had internal space for the bombs, rounded wingtips that added wing span and area, and a slightly larger horizontal tail. Called by the factory the DB-1 (for Douglas Bomber 1), the prototype first flew in April 1935 with two 850hp Wright R-1820 Cyclone radial engines that gave it a top speed of 233mph and cruising speed of 175mph. With a one-ton bomb load it could fly more than 2,000 miles and climb to 25,000ft.

The four-engined Boeing bettered both the Martin and Douglas entries on almost every score save one: cost. This, plus the setback to Boeing's efforts by the crash of their prototype, gave the bulk of the orders to Douglas. In early 1936, the Army Air Corps ordered 82 B-18s, adding another 50 within a few months. Production airplanes used a more powerful version of the Wright Cyclone that put out 930hp.

Once military equipment (e.g. guns, armor plating, radios, etc.) were installed, the empty weight grew such that the performance dropped significantly, leaving it rated at a top speed of 217mph and cruise at only 167, with a realistic range of only 850 miles. But as this was better than any other similar airplane except the B-17, which was moving slowly in the direction of production, deliveries began in February 1937.

The only other production version was the B-18A, which can be recognized by its odd-shaped nose in which the gunner's position extends well forward of that of the bombardier below him.

An order for 177 B-18s was signed in June, 1937, and was soon increased to 255, the most for any US Army bomber to date. All but 38 had been delivered by January, 1940, with the remainder becoming B-23s.

While the Royal Air Force considered the B-18, it decided against ordering any due to what it considered sub-standard performance and insufficient defensive guns. An order for 20 from the Royal Canadian Air Force for what were called the Digby Mk.1 went to their coastal patrol for anti-submarine operations. The only other foreign sales were two that were operated by Brazil for training and then maritime patrol.

The Army B-18s had a limited life as long-range bombers, soon becoming obsolete and being pulled back to the continental USA where they were first used in a defensive role and then on anti-

submarine patrols which resulted in the destruction of two German U-boats. Those still overseas – in Hawaii and the Philippines – suffered greatly from the initial attacks by the Japanese in 1941. The hundreds of B-18s built played a very minor role in combat operations.

The main successes of the Douglas Aircraft Co. during the war were the A-20 Havoc attack bomber (6,278 built) and the SBD Dauntless carrier-based dive bomber (5,936 built). In addition, Douglas manufactured on license almost 3,000 B-17s and almost 1,000 B-24s. Its next twin-engined bombers for the Army were not built until later in the war, when the A-26 Invader and radical-design XB-42 Mixmaster, with its contra-rotating pusher propellers, made their appearances.

Specifications

Length: 56ft 8in
Wingspan: 89ft 6in
Height: 15ft 2in
Wing area: 959 sq ft
Empty weight: 15,720lb
Top speed: 217mph
Service ceiling: 24,200ft
Range: 1,200 miles with 4,400lb of bombs, 800 US gallons of fuel
Maximum bomb load: 6,500lb

Surviving Examples

B-18
USAAC 37-029 – Castle Museum, Atwater, California
USAAC 37-469 – National Museum of the US Air Force
USAAC 37-505 – McChord Museum, Washington State

B-18A
USAAC 38-593 – Pima Air and Space Museum
USAAC 39-025 – National Museum of the US Air Force
USAAC 39-036 – McChord Museum, Washington State

Douglas B-23 Dragon

The last 38 Douglas B-18 Bolos to be ordered were delivered as B-23s, with extensive improvements, yet they still were basically DC-2 airliners ineffectively turned into offensive weapons. It was typical of many pre-war Army Air Corps airplanes, designed for peacetime conditions and lacking sufficient performance, defensive armament and armor protection for the crew. In comparison with its B-18 predecessor, the B-23 still resembled an airliner on a mild regimen of steroids, when completely new and more realistic designs should have predominated.

The B-23 had a few feet greater length, wingspan and height, and more than 3,000lb greater empty weight, compensated for with a pair of more powerful Wright R-2600 Cyclone 14 engines, rated at 1,600hp. It had slightly greater range and much improved service ceiling. It was what would be expected from an airplane that had begun its trip down the assembly line as an obsolescent design. Its only major advancement was the tail turret which carried the first .50 cal. machine gun in an American bomber.

The first production B-23 (there was no true prototype) flew in July 1939, shortly before the war began in Europe. By the end of the year, all 38 had been delivered. Tests showed that it was not what the Army needed nor wanted, lacking the performance and defensive armament that intelligence from Europe had shown was required for a new long-range bomber. Moreover, the design did not lend itself to the major improvements in aerodynamics and power that were needed to bring it up to 1940s standards.

As a result, the B-23s spent a short time patrolling the Pacific coast and were then replaced by more modern airplanes. Many of them then went to training squadrons, while others were converted to UC-67 utility transports in a move back to the airplane's origins. Douglas then moved on to the A-20 Havoc and the A-26 Invader, two of the best light and medium bombers developed during the war.

After the war, many of the surviving B-23s were converted into early executive airplanes with the addition of comfortable seats, tables and appropriate decorations. Thanks to their being kept away from enemy action, at least a half dozen have survived.

Specifications

Length: 58ft 5in
Wingspan: 92ft
Height: 18ft 6in
Wing area: 993 sq ft
Empty weight: 19,090lb
Top speed: 282mph
Range: 1,400 miles with 4,000lb of bombs
Service ceiling: 31,600ft
Maximum bomb load: 4,400lb

Surviving Examples

B-23
USAAC 39-0036 – McChord Air Museum, Washington State
USAAC 39-0037 – National Museum of the US Air Force
USAAC 39-0038 – Commemorative Air Force, Midland, Texas
USAAC 39-0047 – Castle Air Museum, Atwater, California
USAAC 39-0051 – Pima Air and Space Museum

UC-67
USAAC 39-0057 – Fantasy of Flight

Consolidated B-24 Liberator

The common view of those who crewed B-17s was that B-24s were 'the packing crates in which B-17s were shipped'. While the B-24 may have lacked the glamour and visual personality of the Flying Fortress, it was built in greater numbers than any other American military airplane, and exceeded the performance of the B-17 in numerous respects.

Consolidated Aircraft was formed in 1923 by aviation pioneer Reuben Fleet, and well into the 1930s produced military trainers, small flying boats and personal airplanes. It became a significant part of the American aviation industry in 1937 when the US Navy gave it a contract for 60 PBY Catalina flying boats.

Two years later it was asked by the US Army to become a second source for quantity production of Boeing B-17s, but instead preferred to build a brand new design of its own, the B-24 Liberator. B-24s were eventually built by not only Consolidated but also by North American, Douglas and especially the Ford Motor Co. Thus was born a running competition that resulted in both airplanes

being better than they would have been otherwise. Together, more than 30,000 of these heavy bombers were built and Fortresses and Liberators darkened the skies over occupied Europe and scores of Pacific Islands, dropping more than a million tons of bombs and carrying out a wide variety of other assignments.

The prototype XB-24, which flew on 29 December 1939, revealed the shape which would remain unchanged, except for a variety of nose gun emplacements, through to almost the end of the production run. Most noticeable was the high aspect ratio wing with a new airfoil and which offered increased efficiency, higher speed and greater range. Of almost as great significance was the spacious fuselage, which was to be used for carrying large loads of weapons, cargo and people.

The second prototype – XB-24B – flew in 1940. The disappointing top speed of the first was overcome by using turbo-superchargers instead of engine-driven superchargers, thus boosting the maximum speed from 273mph to 310mph.

In 1940, the US Army Air Corps had ordered 43 airplanes for test and evaluation, the French had ordered 120 and the British 164. Some of the British order were to be the first Liberators to see action, in the form of radar-equipped long-range patrol bombers of RAF Coastal Command, starting in the summer of 1941. Even earlier, Liberators were used to start the Trans-Atlantic Return Ferry Service as unarmed transports.

The first American use of B-24s was also in their transport function, carrying VIPs, returning ferry crews and special cargoes to and from the continental United States. Finally, the airplane designed as a heavy bomber got its chance to play its intended role. Several B-24Ds of the first major production run were used in an attack on Rumanian oil fields in June, 1942, followed by a growing number of airplanes operating from bases in the middle East and then from England as part of the rapidly expanding 8th Air Force.

The Pacific Theater of War became the most important for B-24s, thanks to their greater range. They eventually replaced almost all the B-17s in operations against the Japanese. In view of the B-24's adaptability to modifications for other uses, specialized versions began emerging from some of the many factories in which B-24s were being built. The purpose-built C-87 Liberator Express and its US Navy version, the RY-1, entered production, along with the AT-22 advanced trainer, the C-109 Martin-built tanker and the F-7 photo-reconnaissance airplane.

Like the B-17, the B-24 experienced an effort to create a bomber escort bristling with guns. And like the B-17 that was similarly outfitted, the resultant reduced speed and maneuverability ended the project. To aid in fighting off enemy interceptors, Liberators were equipped with a variety of hand-driven and power-operated turrets, eventually settling on the latter.

The first major external change came in 1944, after it had been recommended by the USAAF a full two years before. The characteristic pair of huge vertical tails was replaced by a single tall unit which greatly improved the airplane's handling and stability. After a very few B-24N were so modified, the end of the war meant the end of production for the Army Air Forces. At the same time, orders for an additional 5,000+ were cancelled.

While the successor to the B-17 was the futuristic B-29 Superfortress, the follow-on to the B-24 was a major disappointment. Instead of being innovative from nose to tail like the B-29, the B-32 Dominator was little more than a routine upgrading of the B-24, lacking such modern developments as a pressurized fuselage and remote-control gun turrets coupled to radar. Only a few B-32s saw action. In contrast, hundreds of Superfortresses carried huge loads of high explosive and incendiary bombs directly to the Japanese homeland on long flights from captured island bases and then ushered in the atomic era. Convair would not have another successful bomber program until just after the war, when its enormous six-engined (later 10-engined) B-36 changed many of the accepted concepts of strategic bombing.

Specifications of the B-24J

Length: 87ft 2in
Wingspan: 110ft 0in
Height: 18ft 0in
Wing area: 1,048 sq ft
Empty-eight: 38,000lb
Top speed: 300mph
Range: 1,700 miles at 190mph with 5,000lb of bombs
Service ceiling: 28,000ft
Maximum bomb load: 12,800lb

Some surviving Examples

B-24D

USAAF 41-32908 – Hill Air Museum, Utah

USAAF 42-72843 'Strawberry Bitch' – National Museum of the US Air Force

B-24J

USAAF 44-44052 – Collings Foundation

USAAF 44-44123 – Indian Air Force Museum, New Delhi

USAAF 44-44175 – Pima Air and Space Museum

USAAF 44-44272 – Planes of Fame

USAAF 44-48781 – 8th Air Force Museum, Barksdale AFB, Louisiana

B-24L

USAAF 44-50206 – RAF Museum, Cosford

USAAF 44-50454 – National Aviation Museum, Rockcliffe, Ontario, Canada

RCAF HE773 – Canadian Air Museum

B-24M

USAAF 44-41916 – National Museum of the US Air Force, at Castle Air Museum, CA

USAAF 44-51228 ('44-50493') – Imperial War Museum, Duxford

North American B-25 Mitchell

Prior to late 1936, the struggling young North American Aviation Co. had produced nothing but small orders of single-engined, low-wing trainers for the US Army and Navy and small foreign air

forces. And so when a twin-engined long-range bomber prototype was rolled out for its first test flight a few days before the end of 1936, it was a risky and critical experiment. What would become the XB-21 started off with the usual minor problems but good overall performance, and was expected to be a strong contender for a major USAAC contract. But not even XB-21's superior speed and range could keep the Douglas B-18 from getting the nod, due in great part to its cost being barely half that of its North American rival.

The next serious attempt by North American to build a bomber produced the B-25 Mitchell, considered by many to be the best all-around medium bomber of World War Two. The prototype flew in August, 1940, to be followed two months later by the first P-51 Mustang. By this time, production of North American's AT-6

advanced trainer was gearing up, giving this still-young company a trio of airplanes which were to have a major impact on the war. In total, NAA built more military airplanes than any other American manufacturer. At one time the company employed more than 50,000 men and women.

Early in the Army's test program at Wright Field it was determined that a directional stability problem could be cured by eliminating the dihedral in the B-25's outer wing panels. The resulting slight 'gull' effect was to become one of the identifying features of all subsequent B-25s. Otherwise, the basic shape remained constant, at least until several nose designs were developed for planned increases in firepower.

The first Mitchells to be produced were B-25s, there having been no XB-25. The first to be assigned to a unit were the B-25As, which went to McChord Army Air Field in the summer of 1941 for operational tests. Immediately following America's entry into the war in early December 1941, three squadrons of B-25As took on anti-submarine patrols, with the first sinking of a Japanese sub occurring in late December.

With American public morale at an all-time low, a spectacular plan was put into action in May 1942. Under the leadership of air racing hero Jimmy Doolittle, a special unit was formed for an attack on the Japanese mainland. Intensive tests proved it feasible to operate the Mitchell from a large aircraft carrier, and so 16 B-25Bs and their crews boarded the USS *Hornet* (code named *Shangri La*) and headed west across the Pacific. Low-level bombing attacks were made on Tokyo and other cities, doing little physical damage, but boosting American spirits and upsetting the Japanese feeling of immunity from enemy attack.

Into 1943, Mitchells rolled off the assembly lines in great numbers, with many going to the RAF and Soviet Air Force via the

Lend-Lease program. Others were operated by the US Navy as the PBJ. Almost 250 went to Norwegian squadrons in the RAF.

As the excellent load-carrying capability of the B-25 became established, field modifications began to change its basic make-up. As many as eight .50 cal. machine guns were installed in special 'ground attack' noses. The effectiveness of this boost in offensive power fitted in with the increasing use of the airplane in anti-shipping missions. Soon, B-25Gs were joining the fray with a modified 75mm field gun in the nose. While there were drawbacks to using such a large gun in an airplane, many B-25s were so

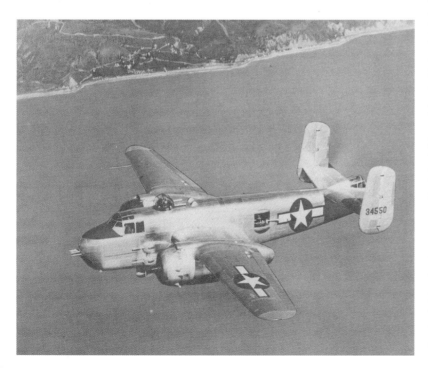

equipped and had the guns removed only when the supply of appropriate targets dwindled. By then, more machine guns were fitted, including two on either side of the front fuselage.

The B-25J was the most widely produced of all the versions, and reverted to the original bomber function. Some of these, operating in the South Pacific, became ground attack airplanes with as many as 18 machine guns, all but three of which were fixed, forward-firing .50s. Still others had additional weapons in the form of 5in air-to-ground rockets mounted on stub wings.

In a very long career, almost 10,000 B-25s were built. Not long after the first B-25 flew, North American began design of a pressurized high-altitude version, which became a completely new design, the XB-28. With a single tail and 2,000hp Pratt & Whitney engines, the first prototype demonstrated a top speed of 370mph. For reasons not completely clear, the plan went no further, though one of the two prototypes sat at Wright Field for many years in full view of passing motorists.

There are at least 100 complete B-25s in existence, though the numbers seem to change almost weekly. They are equally divided between those that are flyable and those that are on static display. In addition, there are dozens whose owners say they intend to restore them to flying or display status… eventually.

Specifications of the B-25J

Length: 52ft 11in
Wingspan: 67ft 7in
Height: 15ft 9in
Wing area: 610 sq ft
Empty weight: 21,100lb
Top speed: 275mph

Range: 1,275 miles with 3,200lb of bombs
Service ceiling: 25,000ft
Maximum bomb load: 4,000lb

Some Surviving Examples

B-25B
USAAF 40-2344 – National Museum of the US Air Force

B-25H
USAAF 43-4999 – New England Air Museum
USAAF 43-4432 – Experimental Aircraft Association Museum

B-25J
USAAF 43-1171 – Imperial War Museum, Duxford
USAAF 44-30423 – Planes of Fame
USAAF 43-27712 – Pima Air and Space Museum

TB-25N
USAAF 4 – Fighter Factory

Martin B-26 Marauder

Martin's sleek Marauder was a big step forward in medium bomber performance. In some ways, it was almost too big a step. In order to achieve the desired performance, the wings were unusually small in relation to the flying weight, necessitating higher than usual take-off and landing speeds for which the average service pilot was not fully prepared. But then, Martin's previous bomber design – the B-18 Bolo – was also a major advancement for its time.

The B-26 was just about the best that could be designed with existing knowledge of aerodynamics and power. Its fuselage was the most aerodynamically clean that had yet been seen, using low-drag turrets and an absolute minimum of parts sticking out into the breeze. To power it, Martin installed a pair of very new 18-cylinder Pratt & Whitney R-2800 Double Wasp engines (the first for any bomber), already rated at 1,900hp and soon to be recognized as one of history's great internal combustion aircraft engines.

So impressed were the Wright Field officials by Martin's detailed presentation that they not merely accepted it but placed an order for 1,100 B-26s long before the prototype had been built, let alone flown. One year later – November 1940 – the first production airplane left the factory without a true prototype having been built. It had single hand-held .30 cal. machine guns in the nose and tail, and a pair of .50 cal. in the first power turret installed on an American bomber.

With close to 4,000hp available, the B-26 could hit 315mph at altitude, but had an unusually high landing speed. As B-26s rolled out and were assigned to service squadrons from early 1941, this became a major problem and the cause of numerous accidents. Several times during the airplane's early history there were serious efforts to cancel it as too risky, and at least once production was suspended by a board of investigation while the airplane's fate was debated. Finally, wiser heads prevailed and after 200 of the original version had been built, an improved B-26 took its place with larger caliber machine guns along with internal equipment changes.

This produced ever-greater take-off weight and even higher landing speeds. Having a positive impact on the B-26's acceptance by service pilots was its impressive behavior in action. In April, 1942, airplanes based in Australia conducted bombing raids on

Japanese-held bases in New Guinea. In May, other B-26s were used to attack the Japanese fleet approaching Midway Island.

Even earlier, the Royal Air Force took delivery of its first improved B-26As which were soon operating in the western desert against Germany's Afrika Corps with an increasing load of fuel, bombs and machine guns. As the B-26B, it was the first widely produced version and the first to carry two fixed machine guns on either side of the forward fuselage.

At last, a concrete move was made to reduce the take-off and landing speeds with the increase in wingspan from 65 feet to 71 feet, and the wing area from 602 sq ft to 659 sq ft for late-model B-26Bs. At about the same time, the armament was increased to 12 .50 cal. machine guns. This, along with other changes, added to the weight and somewhat reduced the impact of the wing enlargement.

Still, there was high-level concern over the landing speed, but even higher officials insisted the B-26 was a very good airplane and kept the production lines moving. It is certainly possible that they could see future bombers and fighters having high wing-loadings/landing speeds and felt it was time for the pilots to learn how to prepare for what was sure to come.

By 1943, Marauders were operating in every theater. In North Africa, they were actually used as long-range fighters, shooting down large numbers of slow, clumsy Ju 52s and huge Messerschmitt Me 323s trying to evacuate German troops who had been chased across the sands of Tunisia. On the other hand, use of the B-26 in low-level raids on targets in occupied countries did not work out well, and so they were switched to tactical targets in more conventional bombing missions.

end of the war and the beginning of the jet age were approaching so fast that such an airplane would have been obsolete before it could enter service.

Specifications of the B-26G

Length: 56ft 1in
Wingspan: 71ft 0in
Height: 20ft 4in
Wing area: 658 sq ft
Empty weight: 25,300lb
Top speed: 283mph at maximum weight and 5,000ft
Range: 1,150 miles with 3,000lb bombs
Service ceiling: 19,800ft
Maximum bomb load: 4,000lb

Before production ended with more than 5,100 built, some were used by the US Navy as the JM-2. The final answer to the question of the advisability of operating the high-speed B-26 can be seen in statistics, which show it with the lowest loss rate of any American bomber.

Like most major airplane manufacturers, Martin was at work on a new airplane to replace the one that was just entering production. In this case, it was the XB-33 Super Marauder, the first version of which was to be larger and with much more power (two Wright R-3350 radials). A steady increase in weight soon made it apparent that not even two of the most powerful engines available could achieve the desired performance. The follow-on XB-33A grew into a rival of the B-29 Superfortress and the B-32 Dominator. While 400 were initially ordered, the contract was cancelled and the two unfinished prototypes were scrapped. The

Some Surviving Examples

B-26
USAAC 40-1370 – Hill Aerospace Museum, Utah
USAAC 40-1459 – Military Aircraft Preservation Society, Akron, Ohio
USAAC 40-1464 – Fantasy of Flight

B-26B
USAAF 40-1501 – Pima Air and Space Museum
USAAF 41-31773 – US National Air & Space Museum

B-26G
USAAF 43-34581 – National Museum of the US Air Force
USAAF 44-68219 – National Museum of the US Air Force

Boeing B-29 Superfortress

Boeing's futuristic B-29 Superfortress had an impact unlike any military aircraft before or since. For much of its combat life, it was used almost exclusively for the saturation bombing of Japanese cities. So that its large formations could be within range of the Japanese islands, the US Navy, Army and Marine Corps' 'island hopping' operations conducted in the Pacific Theater, at the cost of so many lives, were for the primary purpose of providing bases for the B-29 onslaught.

Once B-29s were in range of Japan, their bombing raids reduced city after city to smoking ruins. Faced with what could have been a very costly invasion, B-29s were then used to drop the only two nuclear weapons ever used in war, thus ending, in a matter of days, a worldwide conflict that had cost some fifty million lives.

The true forerunner of the B-29 was not the B-17 Flying Fortress, as one would suspect, but the giant Boeing B-15, nicknamed 'Grandpappy'. The B-15 (originally the XBLR-1) was the largest airplane of its day, with a wingspan of 149 feet and power of four 1,000hp Pratt & Whitney R-1830 14-cylinder Twin Wasps which were supposed to provide a top speed of just under 200mph. While only one was built in 1937 and there was never any serious thought of ever equipping squadrons, it did provide the men at Wright Field and at Boeing with priceless experience of operating a very large bomber.

What eventually became the B-29 started out as a series of Boeing design studies. The first was for a much improved B-15 with double the original horsepower. This was followed by a pressurized B-17 whose fuselage resembled Boeing's Stratoliner. Both failed to attract funding in those days of limited money for aircraft production. Boeing then proposed a big bomber with four Allison V-12s in various arrangements, and others with radial engines buried in thick wings. Not until the Model 334 did the definitive B-29 begin to take shape on drawing boards.

A full-scale mock-up of the 334A was built in December 1939, still two years before America entered the war. After the introduction of a new airfoil and a high-aspect ratio wing in a combination that was predicted to produce a top speed over 400mph, a range of 7,000 miles and a bomb load of 10,000lb for shorter range missions, the B-29 began to appear. After this design was enlarged and more powerful Wright R-3350 engines installed, it was given approval for the construction of two prototypes.

The first prototype B-29 didn't fly until September 1942, by which time plans were well along for building them not only by Boeing, but Bell and Martin, too. Fires and crashes, along with

On 24 November 1944, almost as many B-29s lifted off from hurriedly built runways on a recently captured island in the Marianas chain to bomb Tokyo. It was the first step in a long series of larger and larger raids from islands closer and closer to the Japanese mainland. Raids were either by night without escort, or by day with squadrons of P-51s on the prowl for the increasingly sophisticated Japanese fighters.

Methodically, Japan was blasted, and its fighter defenses reduced to near-impotence, as it became clearer every day that the end of the war was approaching. At last, the cities of Hiroshima and Nagasaki were levelled by single atomic bombs in a disturbing demonstration of what future wars could be.

The B-29 was unquestionably the outstanding strategic bomber of the World War Two. But it wasn't the all-time outstanding strategic bomber, nor even the outstanding piston-engined strategic bomber. The magnificent Northrop B-35 flying wing exceeded the B-29's range, payload, speed and defensive armament. The enormous B-36, contemporary with the B-35, and with four jet engines added to its six Wasp Majors, could top anything previously flown. Even Boeing bettered its B-29 with an experimental XB-44 having four P&W R-4360 engines, which produced some 50 per cent more power, and led to the post-war B-50.

Specifications

Length: 99ft
Wingspan: 141ft 3in
Height: 27ft 9in
Wing area: 1,736 sq ft
Empty weight: 74,500lb
Gross weight: 133,500lb

creation of a complicated system for operating the remote-control turrets, slowed the test program, but the equipping of operational training units proceeded. The initial plan was to use B-29s against both Germany and Japan, but the former was scratched from the list as unneeded, and all operations were set up for the Pacific.

In late 1944, Boeing and Bell began turning out combat-ready B-29s with two .50 cal. turrets on top, two below, and one in the tail with a 20mm cannon in addition to its pair of machine guns. Additional fuel tanks stretched the range with 12,000lb of bombs to 3,700 miles. On 5 June 1944, 100 Superfortresses took off from India and bombed Japanese occupied Bangkok, Thailand, in the airplane's first combat mission.

Maximum speed: 357mph
Range: 3,250 miles with 10,000lb of bombs
Service ceiling: 36,000ft
Maximum bomb load: 19,800lb

Some Surviving Examples

B-29A
USAAF 44-61975 – North East Air Museum
USAAF 44-62070 'Fifi' – Commemorative Air Force
USAAF 44-69729 – Museum of Flight, Seattle
USAAF 44-86292 'Enola Gay' – US National Air & Space Museum
USAAF 44-27297 'Bockscar' – National Museum of the US Air Force
USAAF 44-70016 – Pima Air and Space Museum

TB-29A
USAAF 44-61748 – Imperial War Museum, Duxford

Vega B-34 Ventura

In the early phases of the war, the Allies were desperate for modern, high-performance airplanes to replace those that couldn't cope with the superior aircraft being flown by Germany and Japan. As the time to create and prove completely new designs was several years, their purchasing commissions turned to existing civil airplanes. When the British went shopping for anything that could be turned into a long-range patrol bomber to help protect fleets of cargo ships bringing vital goods from America, they took a close look at a series of high-speed, all-metal airliners that had been built by Lockheed. And they liked what they saw.

The first of these airliners to be 'drafted' into the military was the Lockheed 14 Super Electra, which became the Hudson when it was issued guns, bigger engines, and a bomb bay. While it was hardly the ideal airplane for Britain's Coastal Command, it was a considerable step in the right direction when, in the summer of 1939, it replaced most of the Avro Ansons which had been in service since 1936 and were increasingly showing their age.

Lockheed could see the need for a better airplane to protect convoys from U-boat attacks, and so turned to its Model 18 Lodestar airliner. The first of those had been built from a Model 14 which had been returned to the manufacturer following several crashes in airline service. The prototype of what eventually would become the Ventura was thus a Model 14 with an additional section to the fuselage to accommodate two more rows of passenger seats (or fuel tanks or, later, weapons), and was meant to offer airlines greater economy of operation.

No matter how much better the Model 18 might have been, it was eclipsed by the Douglas DC-3, which was revolutionizing the airline business. The Lodestar wasn't a complete failure, however,

based in the Aleutian Islands for attacks on Japanese bases in the Kurile Islands.

The follow-on PV-2 Harpoon was subjected to so many major changes from the PV-1 (such as a wing increased 25 per cent, from 551 sq ft to 686 sq ft) that it probably should have been given a completely new designation. The changes failed to produce the desired performance improvement, and in fact resulted in a serious wing weakness. The delay in fixing this meant that fewer than 20 per cent of those ordered were delivered by the end of the war when the contract was one of many to be cancelled.

Lockheed's venture into the medium bomber business was not much of a success, in marked contrast to its fighter and transport efforts. Its Vega division was soon absorbed into the parent company and has had little lasting impact. As for the Model 18 Lodestar and its many offshoots, a lot of them reappeared after the war as some of the first expensively outfitted executive transports. Its direct descendant was Lockheed's P2V Neptune, also a maritime patrol airplane.

In addition to those on display or flying, many are stored in various stages of deterioration, and many others were destroyed in crashes, some while transporting illegal drugs.

attracting foreign sales and being adopted by the US military for a variety of uses.

The RAF saw it as a much improved Hudson, with two 2,000hp Pratt & Whitney R-2800 radial engines that produced a cruising speed 90mph faster, while carrying 2.5 times the bomb load. The initial order was for 675 airplanes, the first of which entered service with the British in late 1942. A second order was for 487 Mk.IIs, though most of them were redirected to the USAAF, where they were known (at least briefly) as B-34 Lexingtons.

To add to the confusion, the USAAF's first order, for 550 in 1941, was actually for what was at first called the O-56 armed observation plane. Their final designation was B-37, to recognize an engine change. In late 1941, a bitter inter-service dispute was settled when the Army got out of this game and transferred the order to the US Navy, which called it the PV-1 Ventura. Many were

Specifications

Length: 51ft 5in
Wingspan: 65ft 6in
Height: 11ft 10in
Wing area: 551 sq ft
Empty weight: 19,375lb
Maximum speed: 300mph
Range: 900 miles with maximum bomb load

Service ceiling: 26,300ft
Maximum bomb load: 3,000lb

Surviving Examples

PV-1 Ventura
RAF AJ-311 – Pueblo, Colorado
USAAF 41-38117 – Auckland, New Zealand

PV-2 Harpoon
– US Museum of Naval Aviation
BuAer 37211 – Fantasy of Flight
BuAer 37230 – US National Museum of Naval Aviation
BuAer 37257 – Pima Air and Space Museum
BuAer 37396 – American Military Heritage Foundation, New Palestine, Indiana
BuAer 37492 – North Myrtle Beach, South Carolina
BuAer 37634 – Lone Star Flight Museum

Douglas XB-42 Mixmaster

The Douglas Aircraft Co., of Santa Monica, California, had been one of the mainstays of American aircraft manufacturing since it was founded in 1921 by Donald Douglas. It had supplied the US Navy with single-engined land-based and carrier-based bombers, and the Army with bombers, transports, trainers, observation planes and amphibians. Its products were well designed, well built and generally quite conventional.

And so it was with some considerable surprise that in 1943 the USAAF received an unsolicited proposal for a high-speed twin-engined bomber that had its two engines buried in the fuselage and driving contra-rotating propellers in the extreme tail. Called the Mixmaster (for a then-popular kitchen appliance) it looked like nothing that Douglas had ever built, but the proposal was solid and so in June, 1943, with the war still looking like it could last forever, two flying prototypes were ordered.

The airplane sketched out would have a top speed over 400mph, a bomb load of as much as 8,000lb and an ability to reach targets as far as 2,000 miles away. It was seen as America's 'Mosquito-plus'. The full-scale mock-up passed inspection in September, and the first XB-42 (initially called the XA-42) flew the following May. It met all the promises, and exceeded those in load-carrying, thanks to two late-model, 1,325hp Allison V-1710 engines, each of which turned its own three-bladed propeller via a long drive shaft.

Unlike the Mosquito, the Mixmaster had two remote-control turrets, each with two .50 cal. machine guns, located near the wing's trailing edge, between the flaps and ailerons, and firing aft. They were to be aimed and fired by the pilot; because of its speed, it was felt that enemy attacks from other than the rear were unlikely.

As if to reinforce the initial high opinion of the design, the second prototype flew in August, 1944, and soon made a non-stop dash from California to Washington, DC, at more than 430mph. The future for the novel bomber should have looked very bright, even though the second airplane was destroyed in a non-fatal crash a few days later. Instead, the attention of the USAAF was rapidly shifting to airplanes powered by the exciting new turbojet engines, which appeared to have a greater future. In 1946, Douglas flew a prototype XB-43, which was a turbojet-powered version of the XB-42, but any hope of a production contract for the jet had been sealed, with the nod going to North American's B-45.

Only two Mixmasters were built, one of which survives. Douglas concentrated on its very lucrative airliner business, turning out hundreds of DC-4s, DC-6s and DC-7s. It didn't reenter the bomber arena until the mid-1950s when it built twin-jet A3D Skywarriors for the US Navy and B-66 Destroyers for the US Air Force

Specifications

Length: 53ft 8in
Wingspan: 70ft 6in
Height: 18ft 10in
Wing area: 555 sq ft
Empty weight: 20,890lb
Top speed: 410mph at 23,000ft
Range: 1,800 miles.
Service ceiling: 29,400ft
Maximum bomb load: 8,000lb

Surviving Example

USAAF 43-50224 – US National Museum of the US Air Force

Northrop A-17A

This US Army bomber started out as the third in a series of versatile, high-performance, non-military monoplanes built with the very latest in technology, starting with the 1930 Northrop Alpha, Beta and finally Gamma, which led directly to the A-17. Three Gammas were flown in mid-1930s Bendix Transcontinental Derbies and a fourth was used on Antarctic exploration. A large (for the time) order went to China, one airplane went to the USSR. and at least one vanished into the Spanish Civil War.

The line began with the Gamma Model 2F that became the prototype Army YA-13 with a 710hp Wright R-1820, and then was developed into the XA-16 attack bomber with an 800hp Pratt & Whitney R-1830. It was flown to Wright Field in October, 1934, and was returned to Northrop for extensive improvements. By March, 1935, the Army Air Corps had ordered more than 100 of what had

by then been highly modified and redesignated the A-17. At a mere $19,000 per copy, it was a bargain.

Starting in February, 1936, A-17s were assigned to attack groups at Barksdale Field, Louisiana, and March Field, California. All were powered by 750hp, two-row P&W R-1535 Twin Wasp engines, and armed with four .30 cal. machine guns in the wings and one swivelling .30 cal. in the rear cockpit. A ventral gun mount was tried out but was not installed on production airplanes. The bomb load consisted of 600lb carried in the fuselage bomb bay, and lesser weights slung on underwing shackles.

A year later – in 1937 – the original fixed landing gear A-17s were replaced by 130 retractable gear A-17As which were 15mph faster. But it wasn't long before the airplane's lack of speed, bomb carrying capacity and defensive armament rendered it obsolete and they were put to use as trainers and utility planes. The end came in the early months of the war when the remaining ones were turned over to student mechanics for practice.

It wasn't until well into the war that the Northrop nameplate reappeared, first on a pair of XP-56 pusher-prop flying wing fighters that failed to perform up to standard, and then on many hundreds of powerful, heavily armed P-61 Black Widow night fighters. Soon after, the first of the majestic B-35s flew, as John Northrop's long-term fascination with flying wings came to the fore.

Specifications

Length: 31ft 9in
Wingspan: 47ft 9in
Height: 11ft 11in
Wing area: 363 sq ft
Empty weight: 4,875lb

Maximum speed: 207mph
Range: 650 miles with 650lb of bombs
Service ceiling: 20,700ft
Maximum bomb load: 1,200lb

Surviving Example

National Museum of the USAF

Douglas A-20

It was a light bomber and then a night fighter, though its original version could have been mistaken for a commuter airliner. Such wasn't all that surprising, since it was built by a manufacturer that

was leading the world in modern passenger-carrying airplanes. It was the Model 7, then the DB-7, then the Boston, the Ranger, the Havoc, the Moonfighter, the A-20, the P-70, the BD-2, the O-53 and the F-3.

When the prototype Douglas Model 7B flew in late 1938, it was the first twin-engined, all-metal light bomber aimed at an Army contract. It was also the first airplane of any category offered to the military with a nose wheel, and with interchangeable noses, one transparent (for a bombardier) and the other solid (for machine guns). With a pair of 1,100hp Pratt & Whitney R-1830 Twin Wasp radial engines, it easily topped 300mph and revealed surprising maneuverability for an airplane of its size. To the initial order was added 950 of the DB-7A, a similar airplane powered by 1,600hp Wright R-2600 Cyclone engines.

Observing the early flights were members of a French Purchasing Commission, looking for modern combat airplanes that their own

to survive battle damage stood it in good stead during missions without fighter escort.

The main operational version was the A-20G, of which no fewer than 2,850 were built, almost all with the solid nose in which as many as two .50 cal. machine guns and four 20mm cannon were mounted, in addition to a pair of .50 cal. guns in the power turret just aft of the cockpit. Standard internal bomb load of 2,000lb was augmented by as much as 2,000lb more hanging from under-wing shackles.

Of the total Havocs produced, more than 3,000 went to the USSR. via the Lend–Lease program and were highly regarded by the Red Air Force pilots who had grown accustomed to bare-minimum airplanes which displayed no concern for pilot

industry seemed incapable of designing and producing in quantity and on schedule. They were highly impressed, and soon ordered 100, then another 280. Even without firm American interest, the airplane was on its way.

The production prototype, with 1,200hp Pratt & Whitney Twin Wasps, flew in August, 1939, and by the end of the year all 100 airplanes had been delivered to the French. Due to the rapid advance of the German Army, and the lackluster performance by French military leaders, few of them got into action before France capitulated. The remainder of the airplanes from the first and later orders were turned over to the RAF, along with smaller orders originally intended for Belgium.

While the operation by the USA of A-20s dated back to before the Japanese attack on Pearl Harbor, large-scale operations had to wait until establishment of the 8th Air Force in England in mid-1942, when the A-20C went into action with the first of hundreds of daylight raids on the European continent. Its speed and ability

comfort. Other airplanes went to the US Navy as BD-1s and BD-2s, to the Royal Canadian Air Force and to units of several air forces in exile.

Specifications of the A-20G

Length: 48ft 0in
Wingspan: 61ft 4in
Height: 17ft 7in
Wing area: 465 sq ft
Combat weight: 24,000lb
Maximum speed: 317mph
Range: 1,000 miles with maximum load
Service ceiling: 25,000ft
Maximum bomb load: 4,000lb

Some Surviving Examples

A-20
USAAF – Fighter Factory

A-20G Boston
USAAF 43-10052 – Russian Air Force Museum, Monino
USAAF 43-21709 – Lone Star Flight Museum, Galveston, Texas
USAAF 43-22200 – National Museum of the US Air Force

A-20K
USAAF 44-0539 – Museo Aerospacial da Forca Area Braziliera

DB-7B
RAAF AL907 – RAAF Museum, Point Cook, Victoria

Douglas A-26 Invader

Douglas Aircraft Co., whose DC-3 airliner was becoming famous around the world, found itself deep in the bomber-building business as the US headed inevitably into World War Two. Its trim A-20 Havoc attack bomber was beginning to be greeted with enthusiasm by all but its enemies, while behind the scenes, the manufacturer was designing a considerably larger and more powerful attack bomber as its eventual replacement.

Produced in a variety of versions – medium bomber, ground-support and night fighter – it blurred the lines between what had become accepted notions of bomber categories. With a quick swap of its plexiglass bombardier's nose for a solid nose containing as many as eight .50 cal. machine guns, a bomber became a ground-support airplane, though it could still lift and drop thousands of pounds of bombs. It made such changes with so few compromises in performance that it remained in US service for two more wars.

The prototype XA-26 made its first flight in July, 1942 at what is now Los Angeles International Airport; the test pilot was air racing luminary Ben O Howard. It was intended as the successor to not only the A-20 attack bomber, but the B-25 and B-26 medium bombers as well. With two 2,000hp Pratt &Whitney R-2800 engines and a laminar-flow airfoil, it was faster than Japan's ubiquitous A6M5 Zero fighter. Problems with engine cooling were solved by the removal of propeller spinners and the partial redesign of the engine cowlings. It carried a pair of fixed, forward-firing .50 cal. machine guns, and another pair in either of the remote-controlled turrets. It could carry 4,000lb of bombs internally, and another 2,000lb under the wings.

Due to production and administrative problems, the first Invader bombers didn't reach 9th Air Force units in England until June 1944, and they didn't see action for another three months. By early

1945 there were many squadrons in the Pacific as well as Europe that had converted to A-26Bs and A-26Cs, many of these aircraft having been improved with canopies offering better visibility, along with heavier fixed armament in the nose.

The 47th Bomb Group, which had been active in the latter stages of the Italian Campaign, had its A-26Bs modified with radar and all-over matt black paint for night operations. Over 5,000 A-26s were cancelled at the end of hostilities, but production resumed for the Korean Conflict in 1950, and some were still operational in the Viet Nam War many years later. The last US Air Force A-26 was retired in 1972.

Several hundred A-26s were sold on the surplus market after the war, many of them then being converted into fire-fighting bombers with large tanks for chemicals that could be dropped or sprayed. Others found their way into drug smuggling, and more than a

few were used by small air forces in localized military actions, where one modern, high-performance bomber could mean the difference between victory and defeat. Others were outfitted with plush, comfortable interiors to become some of the first dedicated executive transports. Well over 50 still exist in complete, if not always pristine, condition.

Specifications of the A-26B

Length: 50ft 0in
Wingspan: 70ft 0in
Height: 18ft 6in
Wing area: 540 sq ft
Empty weight: 22,370lb
Maximum speed: 355mph

Range: 1,400 miles with maximum bomb load
Service ceiling: 22,100ft
Maximum bomb load: 4,000lb

Some Surviving Examples

A-26B
USAAF 44-34773 – Musee de l'Air
USAAF 41-39288 – Museo Aerospacial, Rio de Janiero, Brazil
USAAF 41-39378 – Pima Air & Space Museum
USAAF 41-39596 – National Museum of the US Air Force
USAAF 44-34610 – US National Air & Space Museum
USAAF 44-34759 'Reynolds Bombshell' (round-the-world record)
  – Teheran, Iran

A-26C
USAAF 43-22494 – Pima Air and Space Museum
USAAF – New England Air Museum
USAAF 44-35323 – Planes of Fame
USAAF 44-35562 – Boeing Museum of Flight, Renton, Washington
USAAF 44-35733 – National Museum of the US Air Force

JD-1
BuAer 77141 – US National Museum of Naval Aviation (actually
  A-26B, USAAF 41-39215)

Lockheed A-28 and A-29 Hudson

A small island like Great Britain is at the mercy of the sea, not merely because of severe weather, but also because of marauding vessels. As World War Two approached, the latter became of increasing concern. Nazi Germany's re-armament included the building of a large fleet of the most modern submarines, known as U-Boats. The development of effective countermeasures was thus a matter of great urgency.

The RAF's Coastal Command had been equipped with Avro Ansons since 1936, when they had been the RAF's first monoplanes with retractable landing gear. Their cruising radius at less than 160mph was less than 400 miles, which left what soon would become a long stream of vital convoys of heavy loaded ships from America without any form of aerial protection for most of their voyages.

The need for a faster, more heavily armed, longer-range patrol bomber was obvious, and so a delegation was sent to America to see what could be done. The result was the first airplane to be supplied to Britain, when Lockheed Model 14 Super Electra 14-passenger airliners were converted into Hudson reconnaissance bombers. They were retroactively designated A-28 by the US Army.

The first Hudsons were powered by a pair of 1,100hp Wright R-1820 Cyclones, and later by 1,200hp Pratt & Whitney R-1820 Twin Wasps. Unlike Ansons, they were all metal, rather than covered mainly with fabric. The Hudson was faster, had longer range, had more than twice as many defensive machine guns, and carried 750lb of bombs for attacking German raiders.

A 224 Squadron Hudson was one of the first RAF aircraft to shoot down an enemy airplane in World War Two, when a Dornier 18 flying boat was destroyed barely a month after the start of the war. Less than a year later, U-Boat *U-570* was so seriously damaged by the guns and bombs of a single Hudson that it displayed a white flag and surrendered.

The first 800 Hudsons were sold to the RAF under contract, after which Lend-Lease took over. Of the initial batch of the Mk.IIIA

for maritime patrol, and for the same purpose by the Royal New Zealand and Australian Air Forces in the Pacific Theater. Considerably less publicized were the clandestine operations flown by the RAF from England and Burma.

Specifications of the Hudson Mk.I

Length: 44ft 4in
Wingspan: 65ft 6in
Height: 11ft 11in
Wing area: 551 sq ft
Empty weight: 12,000lb
Maximum speed: 245mph
Range: 1,950 miles
Service ceiling: 24,500ft
Maximum bomb load: 1,400lb

Surviving Example

RAAF A16-199 Mk.IIIA – Royal Air Force Museum, Hendon

North American A-36A Apache

North American Aviation's first true combat airplane to roll off the assembly line, after a few hundred trainers (some with a pair of .30 cal. machine guns), had preceded it, had a very confusing early life. The British wanted more Curtiss P-40s, but Curtiss was stretched to its limit. So they approached North America to take on the task. But the British hadn't counted on the pride which led NAA to suggest designing and building a completely new airplane which, they insisted, would be better than any P-40.

version, half went to the RAF and half were taken over by the US Army and called A-29, while others became US Navy PBO-1s. Deliveries to Britain continued with 309 Mk.Vs, and 450 Mk.VIs until they totalled over 2,000 when production ended in June, 1943, and they were replaced on the line by B-34 Venturas. The remaining Hudsons were then used for transport and training purposes.

In British service, most were on the rolls of Coastal Command and spent their long hours in the air searching for U-Boats out of bases in Northern Ireland and Iceland. Sizeable numbers of others bombed enemy installations in Norway, flew photo-reconnaissance missions over many parts of occupied Europe, and even operated as far afield as the Middle East.

American use of the Hudson was mainly limited to training in the AT-18 designation, though some were used by the US Navy

Clearly desperate for fighters, the British acquiesced, and NAA went to work to create an airplane having far greater performance than even its best prior achievement. What later became known as the XP-51 was built in a few months and exceeded anyone's expectations regarding speed, maneuverability and payload. Not completely oblivious to what was going on in its own backyard, the US Amy Air Corps appropriated two of the first dozen to be completed, as the first one to fly was easily out-performing the best current airplanes.

The new airplane soon became known as the Mustang and made more than its share of history. But before that could happen, the USAAC gave NAA its first order for several dozen of the new airplanes... to be used as dive bombers! It was this airplane that suffered (if an inanimate object can be said to suffer) the confusion of three different names, at least one of which apparently was official, or at least semi-official: Apache, Invader, and finally, Mustang. The fighter and the dive bomber were so similar that any one of these names should have sufficed.

The first Mustangs were fitted with the only liquid-cooled, in-line engine then being built in the USA: the new V-12 Allison V-1710, first rated at just over 1,000 hp. The engine's performance degraded rapidly as its altitude increased, so it was only natural that the new aircraft be given an assignment that enabled it to shine at low altitude. And what can be done at lower altitude than dive bombing? But so aerodynamically sleek was the basic airframe that dive brakes that extended from both the upper and lower surfaces of the wings were installed so that a pilot could hold down his speed to the limit set for accurate attacks.

P-51 and A-36 Mustangs were used for dive bombing in many theaters of war, and it hardly seemed to matter which was which. After all, P-47 Thunderbolts and F4U Corsairs were used for dive bombing without anyone foisting new names and numbers on them. So it is difficult to trace the development of the A-36, as its function was assumed by P-51s. But it did its job well. No further developments of the basic airplane can be said to have been created expressly or even primarily for dive bombing. North American had its hands full building AT-6 trainers, B-25 medium bombers and P-51 fighters by the thousands.

Specifications

Length: 32ft 3in
Wingspan: 37ft 0in
Height: 12ft 2in
Wing area: 236 sq ft
Loaded weight: 10,000lb
Maximum speed: 365mph
Range: 550 miles
Service ceiling: 25,100ft
Maximum bomb load: 1,000lb

Surviving Example

USAAF 42-83665 – National Museum of the U.S. Air Force

US Navy

Grumman TBF/TBM Avenger

The Avenger was only the US Navy's second all-metal monoplane intended specifically for launching torpedoes. The first, the Douglas TBD Devastator, in service since 1937, was clearly out of date when the war began, being too slow and carrying too few small-caliber defensive guns. In the pivotal Battle of Midway in May, 1942 few TBDs survived the initial phase.

According to most experts, the Avenger was the finest all-around carrier-based torpedo bomber of the war. It carried a heavy load at good speed, was well armed to fend off attackers, and could withstand considerable battle damage, a quality it had in common with other products of what was cheerfully called the Grumman 'Iron Works' in recognition of a reputation for building heavy-duty structures.

Grumman also knew how to work fast. From the first flight of the prototype XTBF-1 in August, 1941, to its entry into service, a mere five months elapsed. Its first combat – at Midway – was little more successful than that of the Devastator, both of them unable to survive alone while sticking to their low, steady course toward a targeted surface vessel. With reasonable fighter cover, however, the Zeroes could be kept busy and the Avengers were effective.

With Grumman in full production of TBFs. the US Navy wasted no time in getting them to fleet units in the Atlantic, as well as in the Pacific. But more were needed, and Grumman was at its limit with the equally-needed F6F Hellcat Navy fighter. As had happened with other American manufacturers that were better prepared to design warplanes than to build them in the quantities demanded, there was a great need for alternate production facilities.

To meet that need for Avengers, the Navy enlisted General Motors, for many years the world's largest producer of automobiles. GM

responded by creating an Eastern Aircraft Division, building as many as 400 of what were designated TBMs per month. Eventually, more than 7,500 TBMs were built, differing only in minor ways from Grumman TBFs,

With the success of the basic torpedo bomber, it was only logical to expect that other uses would be found. In all, 43 versions were produced, some of them after the war ended. Most important were the TBM-1C (2,336 built), TBF-1 (2,291 built), and various models for the Royal Navy (1,054). Many had radar gear in a large radome on the right wing for use in finding surface vessels. Others were equipped for photo-reconnaissance missions. After the war, a few TBM-3Rs were rebuilt to carry up to seven rather uncomfortable passengers on short hops to and from aircraft carriers.

When the war ended, orders for more than 2,000 TBMs were cancelled.

The first effort to create a successor to the Avenger – the XTB2F – was to have been a twin-engined carrier-based torpedo bomber fitted with no fewer than 10 .50 cal. machine guns. It was determined to be too large to operate from aircraft carriers, and so the XTB3F replaced it. This soon became the AF-1 Guardian, a strictly post-war airplane that bore little resemblance to any version of the Avenger.

Of almost 10,000 Avengers built, more than 150 ended up on the civil market, most of those being bought for use as tankers dumping water or chemicals on forest fires in the American and Canadian west. Others were used to spread chemicals on agricultural crops. At least 60 have survived the decades, with about 25 of those on display in museums and 35 retained in flying condition by private owners, many of them being flown in air shows.

Specifications of TBM-3

Length: 40ft 0in
Wingspan: 54ft 2in
Height: 15ft 5in
Wing area: 490 sq ft
Loaded weight: 15,900lb
Maximum speed: 270mph
Range: 1,215 miles
Service ceiling: 22,400ft
Maximum bomb load: 2,000lb

Some Surviving Examples

TBF-1
BuAer 0628 – US National Museum of Naval Aviation

TBF-1C
BuAer 24085 – US National Air & Space Museum

TBM-3
BuAer – US National Museum of Naval Aviation
BuAer '46214' – Imperial War Museum, Duxford
BuAer 53229 – George Bush Presidential Library and Museum, College Station, Texas
BuAer 53353 – Commemorative Air Force, Midland, Texas
BuAer 53454 – Fighter Factory

TBM-3E
BuAer – New England Air Museum
BuAer 53403 – Nimitz State Historical Park, Fredericksburg, Texas
BuAer 53953 – US National Museum of Naval Aviation
BuAer 69355 – Israeli Air Force Museum, Hatzerim Air Base
BuAer 69472 – Pima Air and Space Museum
BuAer 85890 – US National Museum of the Marine Corps
BuAer 91264 – Planes of Fame
BuAer 91598 – Fantasy of Flight

TBM-3S
BuAer 53503 – Commemorative Air Force, Harlingen, Texas
BuAer 69327 – Imperial War Museum, Duxford
BuAer 85861 – Canadian Forces Base Shearwater, Nova Scotia

TBM-3U
BuAer 53785 – Palm Springs Air Museum
BuAer 69329 – Lone Star Air Museum, Houston, Texas

A.S. Mk.II
BuAer 24336 – Royal New Zealand Air Museum, Wagram

A.S. Mk.IV
FAA XB446, BuAer 69502 – Fleet Air Arm Museum

Douglas SBD Dauntless
The modern era of dive bombing may have begun at the 1934 Cleveland National Air Races, when the US Navy Curtiss F8C Hawk biplane was demonstrated in simulated dive bombing attacks. Among those in attendance was Ernst Udet, a German

World War One ace who became deeply involved in the rebirth of the Luftwaffe, which was supposedly outlawed by the Treaty of Versailles which ended that war. He arranged for two F8Cs to be purchased by Germany and pilots trained in the technique, which would appear when Germany invaded Poland in 1939, when Ju 87 Stukas spread destruction and fear.

The US Navy, through its Marine Corps, was experimenting with dive bombing as far back as 1919. When it received its first purpose-built, though marginal, aircraft carrier, with its obvious limitations on the size and weight of its airplanes, it saw the dive bomber as a way to make the best possible use of the bombs that could be lifted from the short 'runway'.

A dive bomber, at least in theory, should be able to place a higher percentage of its bombs on a target than could an Army bomber dropping more bombs from much higher altitude. In 1926, the US Navy's fleet exercises included dive bombing for the first time. By 1934, the Navy held a design competition for a more modern dive bomber: an all-metal monoplane with retractable landing gear.

With Curtiss not yet in the monoplane bomber business, Northrop won the Navy contract with its BT-1, a descendant of the sleek Alpha mail plane. By the time its shortcomings had been corrected, Northrop had sold that part of its business to Douglas, which redesignated the airplane XSBD-1. In April, 1939, an additional order was awarded for 144 of what became the Dauntless.

A batch of SBD-1s was delivered to the US Marine Corps in June, 1940. Most of the 144 were the much improved SBD-2 with greater range and automatic pilot. Squadrons aboard the USS *Lexington* and *Enterprise* were the first to be equipped, starting in November, 1940. When the Japanese fleet attacked Pearl Harbor a year later, the Marine SBDs were among scores of airplanes destroyed on the ground. A few from the *Enterprise*, then returning to port, got into action, but without fighter protection, did poorly.

A few days later, a Japanese submarine, loitering in the Hawaiian Islands, was sunk by a Dauntless pilot, thus scoring the type's first important victory. Just a few months later, when the Japanese mounted a major assault on Midway Island, it was pilots of the SBDs that dealt the enemy a crushing blow by sinking four of their largest carriers, and causing the loss of hundreds of airplanes which suddenly had no place to land.. The Japanese Navy's carrier force never fully recovered.

From then on, carriers supplied much of the air cover for the island-hopping program upon which the US had embarked. More Japanese carriers were sunk, along with other warships and cargo vessels, as the tide slowly turned in the Allies' favor. Increased crew protection and more guns made the Dauntless an ever-better offensive weapon. At least one Navy pilot – Cook Cleland – became an ace while flying one of these dive bombers, while others held their own while sinking greater tonnage of enemy ships than any other type – Navy, Marine or Army – as well as providing air support for landings on scores of Japanese-held islands.

Design departments of all the major aircraft manufacturers were constantly trying to improve their latest products and to create entirely new airplanes for a war that was changing almost from week to week. The SBD, good as it was, would not remain at the top for long, as enemy airplanes improved and aeronautical technology moved ahead by leaps and bounds. In April 1943, before the SBD had reached its peak, Douglas flew the prototype of its planned two-seat replacement, XSB2D-1. It was larger, much heavier and more powerful, with a 2,300hp Wright R-3350 twin-row radial engine. It was far faster and carried a greater load of bombs.

The Navy ordered hundreds, then changed its mind and the SB2D became the single-seat BTD-1, of which 28 were delivered by the end of the war. Not even an experimental piston-and-jet-powered XBTD-2 could stem the onslaught of pure turbojet combat airplanes, and so the Dauntless line ended with almost 6,000 having been built.

Specifications

Length: 32ft 8in
Wingspan: 41ft 6in
Height: 13ft 7in
Wing area: 325 sq ft
Loaded weight: 10,400lb
Maximum speed: 250mph

Range: 1,345 miles
Service ceiling: 22,525ft
Maximum bomb load: 1,600lb

Some Surviving Examples

SBD-2
BuAer 02106 – US National Museum of Naval Aviation

SBD-3
BuAer 06508 – US National Museum of Naval Aviation
BuAer 06624 – US National Museum of Naval Aviation, at Kalamazoo Air Zoo Museum, Michigan

SBD-4
BuAer 06833 – US National Museum of Naval Aviation, as crashed
BuAer 06853 – Royal New Zealand Air Museum, Wigram, as crashed
BuAer 06900 – US National Museum of Naval Aviation, as crashed, at San Diego Aerospace Museum
BuAer 10518 – Yanks Air Museum, Chino, California
BuAer 10575 – US National Museum of Naval Aviation, at Midway Airport, Chicago, Illinois

SBD-5
BuAer 28536 – Planes of Fame
BuAer 36173 – Patriots Point Naval and Marine Museum, Mt. Pleasant, South Carolina
BuAer 36175 – Palm Springs Air Museum, California
SBD-6
BuAer 54605 – US National Air & Space Museum

A-24A
USAAF 42-60817 – Tillamook Air Museum, Oregon, as SBD-3

A-24B
USAAF 42-54532 – Commemorative Air Force, Cedar Ridge, Georgia, as SBD-3
USAAF 42-54582 – US Marine Corps Museum, at National Museum of the US Air Force
USAAF 42-54682 – Lone Star Flight Museum as SBD-5

Curtiss BF2C-1 Goshawk

When an airplane was neither a pure bomber nor a pure fighter, we'll take its designation as a form of authority; in this instance the BF2C was the second Bomber Fighter type built by Curtiss. Since 'bomber' comes first, we'll categorize it as such for convenience. Curtiss had been building highly successful single-seat and two-seat biplane fighters, scouts and scout-bombers for the US Navy for over a decade, starting with the FC-1 in 1922.

The BF2C started out as the fourth F11C-3 fighter, which had been modified with a retractable main landing gear, which required a deeper forward fuselage for wheel storage. The deeper fuselage added drag, while the retraction mechanism for the landing gear added weight. But Curtiss felt that the increased speed gained by hiding the wheels was worth the trouble.

The final prototype XF11C-3 differed markedly from the first, with metal wings instead of the wooden ones, and a more modern NACA airfoil in place of the conservative Clark Y. The result of all these changes was redesignated the XBF2C-1, which went into production. The US Navy ordered 27 of them with modifications to the turtledeck, cockpit enclosure and lower wing . The aircraft

served until early 1938 when they began to be replaced by more combat-ready Polikarpov I-15s and I-16s.

The BF2C was the last of many types of biplane fighters to be produced by Curtiss, as the next fighter from that company was the low-wing P-36.

Specifications

Length: 23ft 0in
Wingspan: 31ft 6in
Height: 10ft 10in
Wing area: 262 sq ft
Loaded weight: 5,085lb
Top speed: 285mph
Range: 800 miles
Service ceiling: 27,000ft
Maximum bomb load: 475lb

Surviving Example

Thai Air Force Museum (as Hawk III)

Curtiss SB2C Helldiver

Most successful World War Two aircraft experienced some controversy, especially in their formative years. While most of them survived to become recognized for their true worth, others were followed by accusations throughout their active lives and sometimes for years after. So it is with the SB2C Helldiver and its manufacturer, the Curtiss-Wright Corp., both of which have been cast in an unfavorable light well beyond their productive periods.

also carried two .30 cal. machine guns while up to 550lb of bombs hung from the wings.

Starting in late 1934, they were assigned to the aircraft carrier *Ranger*, but only for a few months, as difficulties with the landing gear proved so serious that the BF2C was withdrawn from active service with the fleet.

Export sales of what was called the Model 68 or Hawk III, however, flourished. With the original wooden wings and a 770hp Wright R-1820 engine, 24 were bought in 1935 by Thailand, to be joined by another 50 built on license. Eventually, they were relegated to use as trainers, serving in that capacity until 1949, with one of them surviving to go on display,

Another 102 were bought by the Chinese Air Force and became its main fighter after the Japanese attacked in August 1937. They

The Curtiss-Wright Corp. and its immediate predecessors, may have sold more different aircraft to the American military than any other manufacturer, dating back to the World War One-era JN-4 'Jenny' trainer. The 1930s designs that triggered the great enthusiasm for dive bombing were the Curtiss Hawk II, whose air show displays led to Germany's acquisition of a pair and the subsequent Luftwaffe emphasis on dive bombing, and the Curtiss SBC (the first 'Helldiver'). One suspects that the thrilling sight and scream of airplanes hurtling straight down to plant 'bombs' on simulated targets may have played some role in the decision.

The prototype XSB2C-1 appeared to offer much in the way of performance that the US Navy needed in order to effectively replace the Douglas SBD, which was slipping behind the times. When the prototype first flew in December, 1940, it quickly began to show a series of weaknesses, especially in the area of low-speed stability

and control, which are so vital in aircraft carrier take-off and landing operations, as well as in the final phase of a dive bombing attack. Even before the first flight, wind tunnel tests showed that the stalling speed was so high it would not be able to operate from carriers, and so the wings had to be enlarged by 10 per cent.

The struggling test flying program, with two early crashes, brought the entire manufacturing plan near cancellation, Only the Japanese attack on Pearl Harbor 'saved' the Helldiver, bringing with it an unprecedented demand for all types of aircraft, including those with lingering serious problems. The Helldiver went into production with many of its problems unsolved, the Navy hoping Curtiss-Wright's long experience would get it through some difficult times.

Navy pilots and their leaders were far from pleased with the airplanes they were getting, many of them vocally preferring the Douglas SBD. It took a full 3.5 years after the first flight of the prototype for the airplane to get into combat, whereas Grumman's Avenger torpedo bomber was in action just six months after the type's initial flight. Despite its greater size and power, the SB2C's performance was only marginally better than that of the airplane it was meant to replace.

Curtiss engineers gradually worked out many of the bugs, but still the SB2C was not what the Navy thought it would get. When large numbers of both the SB2C and the SBD took part in the epic June 1944 Battle of the Coral Sea, more than 80 per cent of the Helldivers were lost – mainly by running out of fuel – while only 15 per cent of the SBDs failed to return. The emotional impact on the surviving Helldiver pilots as they contemplated their next missions must have been considerable.

Regardless, the SB2C continued to improve, with more power, a redesigned vertical tail and many less obvious changes. By the end of the war, more than 8,300 had been built, making it the most extensively produced American dive bomber… and the last of that highly specialized type.

Curtiss-Wright was not unaware of the poor design job it had done, and as early as December, 1941, it received a contract to build two prototypes of the follow-on SB3C. It was to have greater range and speed, along with offensive fire power: six fixed .50 cal. machine guns or four 20mm cannon in the wings, plus defensive armament in the form of a power-operated turret aft of the pilot. To lift all this and a bomb load of up to 5,000lb, it was to use a 2,500hp, 18-cylinder Wright R-3350 engine. But as the project moved along, it became clear that it would not have the performance of a rival being designed by Douglas Aircraft.

What had become obvious by now was the manufacturer's steady descent into mediocrity. Attempts to keep the P-40 assembly line going with increases in power and decreases in drag had produced no more than prototypes which were unable to keep up with current airplanes. Early post-war attempts to get into the jet game resulted in the huge, unwieldy six-engined XP-87 fighter for the Army. The world of aeronautics had passed the old-line builder by, and its plants were soon sold off to more creative firms like North American Aviation. A proud chapter ended with few tears shed.

Specifications

Length: 36ft 8in
Wingspan: 49ft 9in
Height: 13ft 2in
Wing area: 422 sq ft
Loaded weight: 16,615lb

Maximum speed: 280mph
Range: 1,100 miles
Service ceiling: 25,100ft
Maximum bomb load: 2,000lb

Surviving Examples

SB2C-1A
BuAer – National Museum of the US Air Force (as A-25A)

SB2C-3
BuAer 19075 – Yanks Air Museum, Chino, California

SB2C-5
BuAer 83479 – US National Air & Space Museum (at US National Museum of Naval Aviation)
BuAer 83321 – Helenic Air Force Museum
BuAer 83589 – Commemorative Air Force, Harlingen, Texas
BuAer 89255 – Lann-Bibone Air Base, Lorient, France
BuAer 83410 – Royal Thai Air Force Museum, Bangkok, Thailand

A-25A
BuAer 75448 – Anoka, Minnesota
BuAer 75552 – Anoka, Minnesota
BuAer 76805 – Anoka, Minnesota

Consolidated PBY Catalina

The concept of the patrol bomber dates back to World War One, when pilots of scout planes spontaneously extended their functions to those of a bombardier by dropping small hand-held bombs at enemy targets they had spotted. While the embarrassing lack of accuracy of such attacks rendered them no more than a nuisance, the idea was planted and steadily improved upon. By the early 1930s, the patrol bomber was a recognized category of combat airplane.

The tale of the Catalina began in 1928, when Reuben Fleet, founder of Consolidated Aircraft Corp. in 1923, failed to sell the US Navy a twin-engined PY-1 flying boat as the appropriations funds were tied up on other contracts. He stuck with the idea and in 1931 managed to convince the admirals that they needed an improved version, the P2Y-1. With a steady stream of improvements, this became the XP3Y-1 which was then redesignated the PBY-1.

The new seaplane offered much better performance, being cleaner (a single central pylon supported the entire wing in lieu of a maze of struts and wires, a single tall vertical tail replaced twin fins and rudders), and could fly much farther in search of enemy vessels upon which to deposit its 2,000 pounds of bombs and depth charges.

Even before the USA was bombed into the war, there was a move to retire the PBYs as the more modern Martin PBM Mariner was coming into service. But the Catalina was such a favorite with its crews due to its long range and ability to absorb punishment and still get them home, that it remained in production through the war.

Even while Catalinas were performing their intended duties, they were found to be highly useful for other functions. They

The amphibian version ('A' suffix) of the Catalina/Canso was one of the few surplus military types that found a large demand in the civilian market, in particular as they were relatively easy to modify to carry water or chemicals to drop on forest fires. About half of today's 30 flyable survivors are in that category, while at least 15 more are on static display, and others are in storage awaiting eventual restoration to flying or display status.

Specifications of the PBY-5A

Length: 63ft 10in
Wingspan: 104ft 0in
Height: 20ft 2in
Wing area: 1,400 sq ft
Loaded weight: 35,400lb
Maximum speed: 175mph
Range: 2,350 miles
Service ceiling: 18,100ft
Maximum bomb load: 3,970lb

Surviving Examples

PBY-5
BuAer 08317 – US National Air & Space Museum, at National Museum of Naval Aviation

PBY-5A
BuAer 46595 – National Museum of the US Air Force (as OA-10), from National Museum of Naval Aviation
BuAer 33993 – National Museum of the US Air Force, at McChord AFB, Washington, as OA-10

served as conventional bombers, especially in the island-hopping Pacific war. And they rescued hundreds of Allied airmen whose original mounts had been shot out from under them and were left adrift in life jackets and tiny life rafts. The 'Cat's' usefulness grew as it was tried in new jobs and did them well.

Gradually, the need for slow, poorly armed flying boats for patrol was taken over by long-range landplanes and by larger flying boats. Yet the Catalinas soldiered on in the service of not only the US Navy, but the Army Air Forces (as the OA-10), and the Royal Air Force, which will always remember it as the seaplane that located the very troublesome German battleship *Bismarck* so Royal Navy Swordfish torpedo bombers could render it impotent. By the time production was ended, more than 3,000 had been built by Consolidated and by two Canadian firms.

BuAer 48325 – Fantasy of Flight
BuAer 08109 – Flyhistorisk Museum, Solo, Norway
BuAer 48419 – Museu Aerospacial, Rio de Janiero, Brazil

PBY-6A
BuAer 63993 – RAF Museum, Cosford
BuAer 46679 – Historic Aircraft Restoration Society, Sydney, Australia
BuAer 64072 – National Warplane Museum, Geneseo, New York

PB2B-2 (built by Boeing in Canada)
BuAer 44248 – Power House Museum, Sydney, Australia

PBV-1 ('Canso', built by Canadian Vickers)
RCAF 9810 – Flygvapnets Museum, Linkoping, Sweden
RCAF 11094 – Canadian Warplane Heritage, Mt. Hope, Ontario

PBV-1A
RCAF 11005 – Imperial War Museum, Duxford

OA-10
USAAF – National Museum of the US Air Force

OA-10A
USAAF 44-34049 – Pima Air and Space Museum

Consolidated PB2Y-2 Coronado

World War Two was a period of change in every element of life and aviation experienced as many important changes as any field. Among those were several that directly concerned the use of patrol bombers. While manufacturers were seeking ways of making them faster, longer-ranging and able to lift ever-greater payloads, others were hard at work to make them unnecessary.

Seaplanes blossomed in an era when only they could lift heavy loads off the surface, and then fly for many long hours while patrolling vital areas. At the same time, they were being made irrelevant by the development of long, hard-surface runways and variable-pitch propellers that acted like a car's multiple gears. If new airplanes could fly from continent to continent, who needed water 'runways' of almost infinite length?

When the PBY Catalina ruled the waves, these modern inventions were in the dreaming stage. But when it came time to replace the Catalina with larger patrol bombers that, at least on paper, could do their job better, the job was being taken over by some new kids. That was the situation in which the PB2Y Coronado found itself.

When America entered the war, the PBY was on the verge of obsolescence, awaiting a replacement that was faster, better armed and could carry larger loads of fuel and bombs. Both Consolidated and Sikorsky entered the competition, with Consolidated's XPB2Y-1 winning out over Sikorsky's quite similar XPBS-1. While both firms had long and praiseworthy records in the flying boat field, the future Coronado won. Due to limited funds for such seaplanes, however, only six were ordered, making the victory rather hollow.

The prototype XPB2Y-1 flew in September, 1937, and immediately revealed serious problems in stability and control that required a completely redesigned tail section. As the production line stepped up, other problems appeared; one, the leaking of fuel tanks, was to plague the PB2Y for much of its service life. As the word spread among Navy aviators, the new four-engined patrol bomber acquired a bad reputation, whereas a particularly good one would

because of its size, some used a battery of solid fuel rockets to boost them off the water. Even so, it just couldn't replace the steady, plodding Catalina.

While the Coronado no doubt had its share of fans, and served its nation well, it was difficult to ignore its uninspiring appearance. While the PBY retained the gracefulness of the majestic old flying boats, the PB2Y looked more than a little like a B-24 Liberator with a ship's hull.

Specifications

Length: 74ft 7in
Wingspan: 110ft 0in
Height: 30ft 1in
Wing area: 1,048 sq ft
Loaded weight: 65,000lb
Maximum speed: 237mph
Range: 2,800 miles

Service ceiling: 20,700ft
Maximum bomb load: 12,000lb

Surviving Example

US National Museum of Naval Aviation

Consolidated PB4Y Privateer

It must have been a bitter pill for the US Navy to swallow, when in 1944 it accepted four-engined, land-based US Army Air Forces B-24 Liberator heavy bombers for maritime patrol. They were

be required to enable it to smoothly replace the PBY, beloved by pilots and crews.

As these problems combined with the reduced need for this type of seaplane, the US Navy and the Royal Navy realized it had qualities that could be put to other uses. The mighty Coronado became a transport, carrying large loads of troops to and from battle zones, and evacuating the most seriously wounded to well-equipped hospitals. Its cavernous fuselage could accept loads of otherwise awkward sizes and shapes.

At the same time, the steadily improved versions were being used more as offensive weapons. With a maximum bomb load of around 12,000lb, including, at times, a pair of torpedoes, a PB2Y-4 could do extensive damage, while protecting itself from interception with 10 .50 cal. machine guns. Easy to overload available and they had the range and capacity the Navy needed. Worse, in late 1944 the Navy had little choice but to order brand new PB4Y Privateers, which had been developed from the reliable, proven B-24. They may have been perfectly good airplanes, but they weren't flying boats and they weren't truly Navy airplanes. While the Germans, Japanese and Italians were the obvious enemies, America's Army and Navy continued to reserve some special dislike and jealousy for each other.

The development of the final version of the Privateer was symbolized by the debate over the number of vertical tails to be used. The first stage after transferring some standard B-24s to the Navy was for Consolidated to furnish the Navy with several B-24s that had been specially modified to meet Navy requirements. One of these was the first B-24 with a single vertical tail, borrowed from a Douglas B-23 Dragon and grafted into place. It failed to do the trick.

Next came a B-24 modified by the Ford Motor Co. at its huge plant near Detroit, where hundreds of Liberators were being built. In this case, the single-unit vertical tail was from another Douglas product, a C-54 transport. This prototype XB-24N flew so much better than previous B-24s that the Army soon ordered more than 5,000. This caused Consolidated to rebel, apparently aghast at the idea anyone would think that a car builder could produce a better bomber than people with decades of more appropriate experience. The Navy was also concerned that the B-24N would eliminate any need for a special maritime version. Political pressure, even in wartime, was sufficiently influential to force cancellation of the plan, and so the B-24N progressed no further than eight prototypes. One could be excused for wondering who was at war with whom!

The B-24N was stretched more than 10 feet longer than the original Liberator, allowing space for a flight engineer and additional electronic

gear. Defensive armament was increased, with a second upper turret, and two novel side turrets, for a total of 12 .50 cal. machine guns. Unusual for a large bomber were the one or two 20mm cannon, to be used for strafing ground targets. Along with several thousand pounds of conventional bombs, the Privateer could carry a pair of BAT glide bombs, each controlled by its own on-board radar and thus a major step towards true guided missiles.

In fact, some PB4Ys carried extensive electronics which could be intended for a variety of specialized missions, including weather reconnaissance, airborne communications, and search-and-rescue homing on small radios carried by individual airmen who had been shot down.

Though just over 700 Privateers were built, they continued in use for many years, including those removed from storage during the Korean War and equipped with air-to-surface radar used in chasing down enemy soldiers sneaking into UN-held territory by night. Others were used as hurricane hunters and as electronic sensors. Finally, some ex-Coast Guard airplanes were converted into civilian airplanes which dropped water on forest fires.

Specifications

Length: 74ft 7in
Wingspan: 110ft 0in
Height: 30ft 1in
Wing area: 1,048 sq ft
Loaded weight: 65,000lb
Maximum speed: 237mph
Range: 2,800 miles
Service ceiling: 20,700ft
Maximum bomb load: 12,000lb

Some Surviving Examples

PB4Y-2

BuAer 59819 – Lone Star Flight Museum, Galveston, Texas
BuAer 59876 – Yankee Air Force, Belleville, Michigan
BuAer 66261 – US Museum of Naval Aviation
BuAer 59701, 59882, 66300 and 66302 (flying) – stored as tankers for Hawkins & Powers, of Greybull, Wyoming

Vought SB2U-2 Vindicator

The US Navy in the mid-1930s was in a state of flux. Did it want to stay with the traditional biplanes, as its generally conservative

admirals preferred? Or was it ready to charge into an unknown future and experiment with monoplanes, as its bitter rival, the Army, was about to do? The pilots were in the middle, with the veterans liking the familiarity and visual strength of two wings and lots of struts and wires, the newer pilots tending towards airplanes with better performance, even if that meant higher landing speeds which could make carrier operations even more hazardous.

This was peacetime, when images of actually meeting enemy pilots in mortal combat were hard to visualize, although such thoughts were becoming ever more real as the leaders of Nazi Germany and Imperial Japan harangued their followers with dreams of expansion and revenge and glory. Still, with its two broad oceans as protection, America was far from convinced it would soon, if ever, be at war.

When the Navy finally faced up to advances in aeronautical technology and began its search for more modern airplanes, it tempered the move with parallel interest in the *status quo*. In 1934, it began a competition for a new dive bomber, giving manufacturers a choice of offering a monoplane and/or a biplane, which Vought, of six entrants, did, building a prototype of each… just in case. All six had the still-new retractable landing gear, even if this often demanded an additional compartment inside which to store the wheels and struts, and which added drag at the same time as retraction reduced it.

Lined up against Vought's XSB2U Vindicator monoplane and its XSB3U biplane were biplanes from Curtiss, Grumman and Great Lakes, and monoplanes from Brewster and Northrop. As it turned out, the Navy awarded production contracts to Vought for its SB2U, Brewster for its XSBA-1 Buccaneer, Curtiss for its XSBC-3 Helldiver and Northrop for its XBT-1.

The Vindicator was the best of the lot, not counting the BT-1 which eventually became the Douglas SBD Dauntless. But the Vindicator was a peacetime airplane, with a single hand-held .50 cal. machine gun operated by the man in the rear-facing second seat; a second machine gun was fixed to fire forward. Its bomb load was 1,000lb. Its main characteristics preventing it from becoming an important type were its limited power from an 825hp Pratt & Whitney R-1535 radial engine, and unimpressive maneuverability.

The prototype flew in April 1936, and led to a typical peacetime US Navy order for just 74 airplanes of several versions. Navy squadrons equipped with SB2U-1 and SB2U-2 operated off several carriers, starting in December 1937 and ending in September 1942. They were in combat during the early part of the Pacific war, including the Battle of Midway, but did not fare well in comparison with the SBD Dauntless.

The US Marine Corps operated 57 SB2U-3 built expressly for their land-based units, retiring them by mid-1943 when better airplanes became available.

A version of the SB2U-2, called the V-156-F, was ordered by the French, who planned to fly them off at least one carrier. When the carrier proved too slow for safe take-offs and landings, the Vindicators became land-based. Those thrown into battle against the Germans soon showed their shortcomings, though others flown against the Italians did better against lesser opposition.

A second French order was shifted to the British (where it was known as the Chesapeake) after the fall of France. Despite extensive changes demanded, the airplanes were determined to have too little speed and maneuverability, and were relegated to non-combat duties.

Specifications

Length: 34ft 0in
Wingspan: 42ft 0in
Height: 10ft 3in
Wing area: 305 sq ft
Empty weight: 5,635lb
Maximum speed: 243mph
Range: 1,120 miles
Service ceiling: 20,700ft
Maximum bomb load: 1,000lb

Surviving Example

BuAer 1383 – US National Museum of Naval Aviation

Martin PBM Mariner

If the classic PBY Catalina had the trim lines of a ballerina, its replacement, the PBM, was shaped more like a Sumo wrestler. Ballerinas evoke feelings of graceful motion and perfect timing, in contrast to the wrestler's slow, steady, irresistible strength. If you were going into battle, which one would you prefer to have at your side?

The first of the Mariners to fly could almost qualify as 'cute', being a 3/8-scale model, complete with a real pilot. Using a technique rare among aircraft designers, the Martin engineers built a miniature test version, powered by their version of a 120hp air-cooled Chevrolet Aircraft Co. engine, buried in the fuselage and driving two propellers via belts. Using it, they learned enough about water handling and the take-off and landing characteristics to justify proceeding with the full-size PBM.

The purpose of the PBM was to replace the classic PBY with a seaplane that had greater range and could carry a bigger load of weapons at higher speed, and more effectively fight off enemy airplanes and ships. The first full-size XPBM-1 had a pair of 1,600hp Wright R-2600 radial engines and flew in February, 1939, well before the start of the war. Problems arose in the areas of water handling and flight characteristics, most of which were solved with some redesign of the hull and the increase in tail dihedral.

The first of 20 PBM-1s was delivered to the fleet in September, 1940, carrying five .50 cal. machine guns and with the bomb bays in the engine nacelles. They were used for coastal patrol and what were called 'neutrality patrols' as far from the mainland as Iceland. Once America entered the war, the PBM-1s and new PBM-3s with more power and a stretched fuselage, guarded the Atlantic and Pacific coasts against Axis submarines.

The first version to carry anti-ship radar was the PBM-3C, which had a large, drag-producing radome behind the cabin. Engine troubles plagued the Mariner fleet until 1944, when the Wright engines were replaced with much more reliable 2,000hp Pratt & Whitney R-2800s, creating the PBM-5 which accounted for half the total production of 1,344.

Early in 1944, Martin introduced its XP4M-1 Mercator, a twin-engined patrol bomber design intended for the very specific role of laying mines in the waters surrounding Japan. In any case the first P4M didn't fly until 1946, and the first delivery of a production airplane wasn't until 1949. It was never built in quantity, as the Lockheed P2V turned out to be far ahead in development, and considerably less expensive.

When the war ended, PBYs found civilian occupations, while PBMs stayed in naval service until the mid-1950s, taking part in combat patrol missions during the Korean War. They were eventually replaced by the Martin P5M Marlin, while surplus PBMs went to the Royal Netherlands Navy. Others served on with the US Coast Guard on search and rescue roles.

Specifications

Length: 80ft 0in
Wingspan: 118ft 0in
Height: 27ft 6in
Wing area: 1,408 sq ft
Loaded weight: 58,000lb
Maximum speed: 198mph
Range: 2,135 miles
Service ceiling: 16,900ft
Maximum bomb load: 4,400lb

Sole Surviving Example

PBM-5A
BuAer 122071 – US National Museum of Naval Aviation, at Pima Air and Space Museum

Douglas BTD-1 Destroyer

As the USA found itself preparing for a war that seemed inevitable, the pace of progress in airframes and engines accelerated. Even before Douglas' SBD Dauntless had proven itself in the Battle of Midway, its replacement was in the works. The Douglas XSB2D-1 was a two-seat dive bomber intended to make not only the SBD but the newer SB2C Helldiver and every other dive bomber obsolete.

Two prototypes of what became known as the Destroyer were ordered by the US Navy as early as June 1941. To propel a heavier airplane carrying a greater bomb load, it would be powered by a 2,300hp Wright R-3350 Cyclone 18 engine. To protect itself from enemy fighters which had so far proven a major problem for American dive bombers, it was equipped with two wing-mounted 20mm cannon, and two .50 cal. machine guns in each of two remote-controlled turrets.

Happy with its performance and potential, the US Navy ordered more than 350 SB2Ds in April 1943. The Navy then decided it preferred single-seat dive bombers without the complications of powered gun turrets, and cancelled the rest. Douglas promptly deleted the turrets and the second crewman, and built 28 BTD-1s. The first of these flew in March, 1944, by which time the Navy's needs for the increasingly successful Pacific war were changing even more.

None of the 28 BTD-1 delivered saw action. Douglas, one of the most experienced of all the world's manufacturers, saw the long-term potential of the BTD-1 and developed it into the AD-1, which became the A-1 Skyraider, one of the all-time great multi-role, single piston-engined combat airplanes.

Specifications

Length: 39ft 7in
Wingspan: 45ft 0in
Height: 17ft 7in
Wing area: 373 sq ft
Empty weight: 11,560lb
Maximum speed: 344mph
Range: 1,480 miles

Service ceiling: 23,600ft
Maximum bomb load: 3,200lb

Surviving Example

BuAer 4959 – Wings of Eagles museum, Elmira, NY

Lockheed P2V Neptune

Until 1944, American Navy patrol bombers had been either slow flying boats or highly modified land-based heavy bombers such as the Consolidated B-24s that became PB4Y Privateers. Then came Lockheed with its P2V Neptune, a landplane designed from the

start for maritime uses. It was, to some extent, the descendant of Lockheed's Hudson and Ventura patrol bombers that had been developed from small airliners. They had done yeoman's work in protecting Atlantic convoys from German U-boats when operating from northwestern Scotland, Iceland and eastern Canada, though the Neptune had a look all its own.

The Neptune was offered to the US Navy in late 1942 as a specialized airplane that would carry a much heavier load of bombs and depth charges over a greater range, along with the latest forms of detection equipment. In February 1944, two prototypes were ordered, and in May 1945 the first one flew. It was faster than any of its predecessors, and, for such a large airplane, surprisingly maneuverable.

The XP2V-1 was powered by a pair of 2,300hp Wright R-3350 Cyclones and was armed with six .50 cal. machines, two each in the nose, top and tail turrets. The weapons load was 8,000lb of bombs, or up to 12 depth charges or even two torpedoes in the large bomb bay and/or slung from wing shackles. Search radar was carried under the nose.

The first P2V-1 was delivered to the Navy early in 1946, and the third airplane brought the Neptune to public attention. In early October 1946, a specially lightened and then overloaded airplane named the 'Truculent Turtle' took off from Perth, Australia, and landed at Port Columbus, Ohio, after having flown 11,236 miles in just over 55 hours. The old straight line distance record had been 7,916 miles, set a year earlier with a Boeing B-29 Superfortress. The P2V's mark would stand for more than 15 years. The message had surely gotten through to the USSR that the US Navy would be capable of chasing its growing submarine fleet.

While the P2V came along too late to see action in World War Two, it served longer than most, with the last ending its days with the US Navy in 1972, having served during the Korean and Vietnamese Wars in a wide variety of functions, including spy missions over Soviet territory. The Japanese operated Kawasaki-built P-2Js as recently as the 1980s. Lockheed eventually replaced the Neptune with yet another patrol bomber based on a successful civil airliner, the turboprop-powered Electra.

Many of the civilian survivors among the 1,200 P2Vs built were eventually modified to carry heavy loads of water and chemicals for fighting forest fires, mainly in the American West. Some of these have been preserved, though not in their original military form.

Specifications

Length: 77ft 0in
Wingspan: 100ft 0in
Height: 28ft 0in
Wing area: 1,000 sq ft
Empty weight: 41,550lb
Maximum speed: 314mph
Range: 4,130 miles
Service ceiling: 24,700ft
Maximum bomb load: 8,000lb

Surviving examples

P2V-1
BuAer 89081 'TruculentTurtle' – US National Museum of Naval Aviation
BuAer 147957 – Pima Air and Space Museum

Brewster SB2A Buccaneer

The highlight of the career of the SB2A came before its very first test flight in June, 1941. So promising did the airplane appear that more than 1,000 had already been ordered by the British, the Dutch and the US Navy. Unfortunately, it was all downhill after that, with extensive difficulties with its handling characteristics and production problems delaying its availability until long after its rival, the Curtiss SB2C Helldiver, had established its reputation.

It wasn't just the Buccaneer that had problems: it was that the Brewster Aeronautical Corp. became a textbook example of 'how not to run an airplane manufacturer'. Its first World War Two project was the F2A Buffalo pursuit, which the US Navy initially preferred to the earliest version of Grumman's F4F Wildcat. By the time a few Buffaloes were in action, their many weaknesses had rendered them sitting ducks for the far more nimble Japanese fighters. Adding to the difficulties were labor/management disputes that forced the Navy to take over the plant and fire a couple of shady salesmen who promised more than the factory could deliver.

The final production airplane to come from the Warminster, Pennsylvania, plant was the F3A, a license-built Vought Corsair fighter. Its construction was so mismanaged that not one was accepted by the Navy. It was to have been followed by the XA-32 single-seat dive/torpedo bomber armed with four 20mm cannon, but that never got beyond the prototype stage.

The Buccaneer was not only a rival of the SB2C, it was eerily similar in appearance, having almost the same size and similar performance. Both were powered by the Wright R-2600 radial engine which developed 1,700 hp. The Buccaneer had a turret just forward of the vertical fin with two .30 cal. machine guns in addition to the four .30s in the leading edges of the wings.

Armament consisted of two fixed .30 cal. machine guns in the wings, two .50 cal. machine guns fixed in the fuselage, and two more .30 cal. operated on a flexible mount from the back seat. Up to 1,000lb of bombs could be carried internally.

By the time the most important of the airplane's problems had been solved, the need for the SB2A had passed, and most were used for training and other non-combat services.

Specifications

Length: 39ft 2in
Wingspan: 47ft 0in
Height: 15ft 11in
Wing area: 379 sq ft
Empty weight: 9,920lb
Maximum speed: 273mph
Range: 1,680 miles
Service ceiling: 24,900ft
Maximum bomb load: 1,000lb

Surviving Example

Pima Air and Space Museum (re-painted as USAAF A-35)

More than 1,000 were built, 750 being ordered by the British as the Bermuda and powered by the 1,700hp Wright R-2600 engine. Of the 140 for the US Navy, 80 were the type SB2A-2 with non-folding wings, and 60 were the SB2A-3 with folding wings and arrestor hooks, even though the airplane was never accepted for carrier operations. An additional 160 were ordered by the Netherlands but requisitioned by the US Navy when that country was occupied by Germany early in the war. A version powered by the 2,000hp Pratt & Whitney R-2800 engine was developed for the USAAF as the A-32 land-based dive bomber. Only two prototypes were built, while not one of the intended follow-on – the A-34 – was built.

Chapter 2

Great Britain

deHavilland 98 Mosquito

When most combat airplanes earn praise for their versatility, it is almost always the result of necessity. The post-design need for a high-altitude photo-reconnaissance airplane may be filled by an interceptor upon the installation of cameras. Then the original airplane finds itself lugging two huge streamlined auxiliary fuel tanks which turn it into a long-range bomber escort. These and other changes depend, of course, on the original airplane's adaptability.

In the case of the Mosquito, it emerged as a fully grown versatile fighting machine. Its parallel use as both a fighter and a bomber dates back to the very first production contract, which called for almost equal numbers of either version, along with a couple of dedicated photo-reconnaissance versions. A multitude

of additional uses followed as the airplane displayed its superior capabilities in action.

The origins of the 'wooden wonder' can be found in deHavilland's hurriedly designed and built trio of Comet Racers, which easily won the 1934 England-to-Australia air race. The sleek machines combined then-new retractable landing gear and an unusually streamlined airframe with limited power (a pair of 200hp Gypsy straight-sixes) into an airplane that had almost futuristic performance, cruising at 200mph for many hours.

The formula led to the beautiful Albatross airliner, and then to the dream of a lightweight bomber which would have no peers in combat and would require only a minimum of strategic materials in its construction. Powered by a pair of Rolls Royce Merlin V-12 engines whose power would steadily grow from just over 1,000hp to double that figure, its performance grew to maintain its superiority over anything remotely similar.

The lack of official interest in an unarmed bomber built from supposedly superseded materials almost caused its cancellation, but the prototype, which first flew in November, 1940, displayed a degree of speed and maneuverability that made it clear that deHavilland had created a highly effective fighting machine despite its novel nature. Even those who insisted on sticking with out-dated ideas were forced to admit that it was a worthwhile experiment, since it used little in the way of critical materials in its construction. Showing even more foresight, deHavilland had designed the Mosquito for easy transition from a bomber to a fighter or a photo-plane, one example of each comprising the first three to be built.

The RAF received its first production Mk.I in the summer of 1941, and had it in action by September, when an attempt by several Messerschmitt 109s to intercept one on a photo mission was easily foiled. Many more such missions followed quickly, no doubt to the great consternation of the Luftwaffe, which was still accustomed to having its way over all of occupied western Europe.

With major parts being built by small and medium-size furniture factories scattered around the British Isles and thus almost impervious to large-scale bombing raids, Mosquito production rapidly escalated. The first bomber version to see quantity production was the B.Mk.IV, with -20 series Rolls Royce Merlin engines, and bomb loads increasing from 1,000lb to 2,000lb and soon to 4,000lb. They replaced the Bristol Blenheim, starting with their first operations in May 1942.

Due to their speed and maneuverability, along with the natural radar invisibility of wood, Mosquitoes were used for raids requiring them to get in, drop their bombs and high-tail it out before the German defenses could be brought to bear. Among the lightning daylight raids that so boosted the airplane's mystique were the attack on Gestapo headquarters in Oslo, Norway, which proved of great value to the resistance, and the disruption of a speech to a huge parade in Berlin by Luftwaffe commander Hermann Goering, both in early 1943.

These 'nuisance raids' were followed by the establishment of the Pathfinder Force, elements of which preceded massed formations of heavy bombers to pin-point the main targets with color-coded flares. After quickly jettisoning its bomb load, the Pathfinder Mosquitoes had the speed and maneuverability of fighters, though not the offensive armament, and certainly not the defensive armament. One of the last major uses of the novel bomber was in attacks on V-1 'buzz bomb' launching sites on the French coast, thus easing the stress on residents of southern England.

The demand for Mosquitoes was so great that production facilities were arranged in Australia and Canada, and even planned for the USA. By the end of production around V-J Day, almost 5,600 'Mossies' had been built.

Late in the war, the follow-on to the Mosquito was introduced,. The outstanding (but still mostly wooden) dH.103 Hornet was a smaller, lighter, cleaner, more powerful version that was too late to have any impact on the war, but was operated post-war. Sadly, not a single example of this fastest twin-piston-engined fighter/bomber has survived.

Specifications of the Mosquito B.Mk.XVI

Length: 40 6in
Wingspan: 54ft 2in
Height: 12ft 6in
Wing area: 454 sq ft
Empty weight: 15,510lb
Maximum speed: 408mph
Maximum range: 1,870 miles with 1,000lb bomb load
Service ceiling: 37,000ft
Rate of climb: 15,000ft in 7:45

Surviving Examples

RAF W4050 prototype – deHavilland Aircraft Heritage Centre

B.20

KB336 – Canadian National Museum

TT.35 (modified from B Mk.35)
RAF RS709 – National Museum of the US Air Force
RAF RS712 – Experimental Aircraft Association Museum
RAF TA634 – deHavilland Aircraft Historical Centre
RAF TA639 – RAF Museum, Cosford
RAF TH998 – US National Air & Space Museum
RAF TJ138 – RAF Museum, Hendon
RAF TA719 – Imperial War Museum, Duxford

Vickers Wellington

The Wellington could easily have been a failure, what with a nickname like 'Wimpy' and a novel style of construction called 'basket weave'. But more practical minds prevailed and more than 11,000 were produced, making it one of the more successful types of the early part of the war.

'Wimpy' came from a character in the 'Popeye' comic strip whose middle name happened to be Wellington, and looked even chubbier than the bomber. The 'basket weave' construction proved to be unusually light and yet highly resistant to combat damage. Moreover, it was easily the best bomber in squadron service when the war began.

The method of construction, called 'geodetic', goes back to 1929 and the R100 dirigible, designed by future star engineer Barnes Wallis. It consisted of many short strips of aluminum alloy in a crisscross arrangement that transferred loads to other pieces in order to stabilize the forces. The first airplane to use this system was the Vickers' Welleseley, a single-engined bomber whose best-known achievement in those mid-1930s peacetime years was the setting of the World's Absolute Distance record by two of them together on a 7,162-mile flight from Egypt to Australia in 1938.

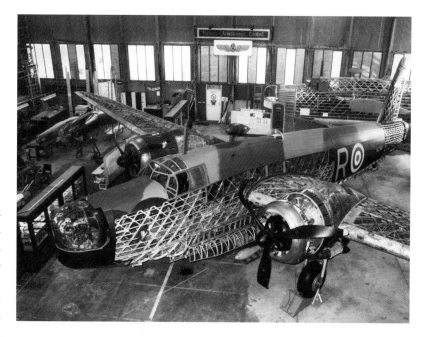

By then, the prototype of what became the Wellington had flown and then been developed into the Mk.I, for which a contract for the construction of 180 had been signed. The plan to power them with the steam-cooled V-12 Rolls Royce Goshawk had been dropped in favor of the more conventional (and resistant to damage) 850hp Bristol Pegasus sleeve-valve radial. This would not be the last change in engines – as production grew, the airplane became heavier and carried a greater load. The first production airplanes were actually powered by 18-cylinder Pratt & Whitney R-2800 Double Wasps.

At about the same time, Vickers was working on its Warwick, similar in appearance to the Wellington, but larger, heavier and thus requiring more powerful engines. Delays in developing new engines retarded progress on the Warwick, which had been intended as a parallel development to the Wellington.

By the time war with Germany had begun, RAF Bomber Command had six squadrons of Wellington Mk.I, 14 of whose airplanes were in action on the second day of hostilities. While its power-operated gun turrets provided much better protection against enemy fighters than did hand-operated machine guns, it soon became apparent that daylight raids by unescorted bombers were simply too risky, and so they consequently were used almost exclusively for night raiding.

As hundreds of Wellingtons became thousands, the knowledge accumulated during operations, along with the realization that the airplane could do more than first expected of it, caused heavier and heavier loads to be lifted, up to 4,000lb block-buster bombs. In the maritime reconnaissance role, some Coastal Command Wellingtons carried a 48-foot metal loop which used a magnetic field created by running electricity through it to explode magnetic mines.

Among the experimental versions of the Wellington were those used to develop a high-altitude bomber. While not completely successful, knowledge gained in solving a long list of engineering problems including cabin pressurization, was of considerable value in the design of later British airplanes. Even if a high-altitude Wellington could have been perfected, German progress in operating its fighters as high as 40,000ft would have cancelled out the Vickers airplane's improved performance.

More than 500 of the similar Warwick were built, but none was used as a bomber, as that role had been taken over by the far more capable heavy bombers: Lancaster, Halifax and Stirling. Warwicks were shifted to duty for air-sea rescue and even transporting men and equipment.

Specifications for B Mk.X

Length: 64ft 7in
Wingspan: 86ft 2in
Height: 17ft 6in
Wing area: 753 sq ft
Empty weight: 18,555lb
Maximum speed: 235mph
Range: 2,200 miles with 1,500lb of weapons
Service ceiling: 22,000ft
Maximum bomb load: 4,500lb

Surviving Examples

Mk.IA
RAF N2980 – Brooklands Museum

T.Mk.10
RAF MF628 – RAF Museum, Hendon (under long-term restoration at RAF Cosford)

Handley Page Halifax

Handley Page's experience with dedicated bombers can be traced back to the very beginning, with the end of the era when any pursuit or scout that had space for a few hand-held bombs was, in effect, a bomber, albeit one that was highly inaccurate and thus had little impact. It was obvious that an airplane designed specifically for carrying more and heavier bombs for ever greater distances was desperately needed. And that was when aerial warfare made the inevitable transition from dueling to destruction.

The first true bomber was the Handley Page O/100, designed for the Royal Navy and produced in small numbers until the much improved O/400 came along. With this airplane, the Royal Flying Corps initiated night bombing raids and strategic bombing by large (for the time) formations of as many as 40 airplanes. These twin-engined airplanes gave good service until replaced, too late to see combat, by the Handley Page V-1500. With its four 375hp Rolls Royce Eagle V-12 engines, it could carry up to 7,500lb of bombs, including a 1,750lb heavy bomb.

Handley Page then reverted to twin-engined bombers through the 1920s and early 1930s, culminating in the open-cockpit, fixed landing geared, heavily-strutted Heyford which entered service in 1933 and didn't completely give way to the far more modern Vickers Wellington until 1939. By then, the prototype Halifax had flown, having grown from the twin Rolls Royce Vulture-powered H.P.56 into the four-engined Halifax, powered by the soon-to-be ubiquitous Rolls Royce Merlin V-12. Before the second prototype had flown, plans were already taking shape for the construction of at least 500.

In March, 1941 and just two nights after the Halifax received its baptism under fire, six B.Mk.Is became the first heavy bombers to attack Germany, when bombs were dropped on Hamburg. Day operations began in June, with both day and night raids continuing until late 1941, when losses to German fighters made daytime ops too dangerous until long-range escort fighters could be developed.

The B.Mk.II soon entered service, but the steadily increasing weight and drag (especially the bulbous dorsal turret) lowered performance below an acceptable level. What followed was the

B.Mk.I Series Ia, with a blown Plexiglas nose in place of another draggy gun turret, and more powerful Merlin engines, boosting the airplane's speed and durability.

Improvements followed throughout 1942, with first the H2S radar bombing system, and then tests with heavier and heavier types of bombs and bomb loads. The Halifax III appeared in 1944 with 1,600hp Bristol Hercules radial engines. These permitted considerable growth in take-off weight, higher cruising speed and bomb loads as great as 14,500lb. Until the Mk.II entered service, Halifaxes had suffered excessively from enemy fighters which found them easy targets due to their lack of speed and service ceiling.

The Mk.IV was the final bomber version of the Halifax, and was aimed at long-range operations in the Pacific when fighting ended in Europe. By then, however, the need for the Halifax ended when it became clear that the job was being done so much more effectively by the fast, high-flying, well-defended Boeing B-29. The Halifax continued to be used for special purposes, including anti-shipping patrol, dropping of supplies, and even serving as a transport.

By the end of production in 1945, almost 6,200 had been built by a half dozen different factories. With the Halifax, Handley Page had built its last piston-engined bomber. The next bomber to carry the much-honored name was the Victor, which used a quartet of turbojet engines to carry nuclear weapons at well over 500mph.

Specifications of the Mk.II

Length: 70ft 1in
Wingspan: 98ft 10in
Height: 20ft 9in
Wing area: 1,275 sq ft

Empty weight: 33,860lb
Maximum speed: 265mph
Range: 980 miles with maximum bomb load
Service ceiling: 22,800ft with R-R engines
Maximum bomb load: 14,400lb

Surviving Examples

Mk.II
Canadian Air Force Museum, Ontario

Mk.IIR
RAF W1048 – RAF Museum, Hendon

Mk.III
Composite airframe – Yorkshire Air Museum, Elvington

Avro Lancaster

The RAF's two outstanding four-engined heavy bombers – the Halifax and the Lancaster – both began life as medium bombers with two Rolls Vulture engines having 24 cylinders in a highly experimental 'X' arrangement. As Rolls Royce was understandably putting maximum effort into its more conventional V-12 Merlin, the Vulture never emerged from a trouble-plagued youth into maturity. With the twin-engined bombers failing to measure up, their four-engined progeny went into mass production and soon into the history books.

Avro's Manchester was to have been part of the RAF's rapidly modernizing strategic bomber force, with a size, range, capacity and speed well beyond anything previously seen. The first one flew in July, 1939, a few weeks before the start of the war. Production plans were put into motion, with 200 and then another 300 ordered, the first being delivered in the summer of 1940. The first use of Manchesters came in a raid on Brest, France, in February, 1941, and soon they were taking part in mass raids alongside other types.

But the Vulture was proving highly unreliable, a serious problem in an airplane with but two engines. The last mission for any Manchester was in June, 1942, after which it was demoted to support operations.

In its place emerged what was first called the Manchester Mk.III, but which had four Merlin engines and was soon to be named the Lancaster. While the fuselage remained effectively the same, the wingspan grew from 90 to 100 feet and the area accordingly, giving an increasingly heavy airplane quite good performance. But it was the reliability of its Merlin engines that produced the greatest gain, much to the delight of mission planners as well as aircrew and their families back home.

As the design of the Lancaster was being created out of the unsuccessful Manchester, Avro was developing a similar airplane in parallel, this turning out to be the York four-engined military transport. So that Avro could concentrate the bulk of its efforts on the much-needed Lancaster, the York received a lower priority, as the RAF decided to rely on American manufacturers for transport airplanes. Twin-engined C-47 Dakotas were available in large numbers, and would soon be joined by the four-engined C-54.

The already-large Manchester bomb bay was steadily modified to accept heavier and heavier bombs, from 8,000-pounders to 12,000lb monsters and finally the 22,000lb 'Grand Slam' bomb. So great was the demand for Lancasters that other firms were soon brought into the system, including Vickers-Armstrong, Armstrong Whitworth and even Austin Motors.

First to put the Lancaster into action was the RAF's 44 Squadron, which used them to lay mines in March, 1942. Its first bombing raid followed a few months later with a raid on a German factory building U-boat engines. As production grew, so did concern that Rolls Royce might not be able to supply all those coming off the assembly lines. Several hundred Lancaster II therefore were built with Bristol Hercules radial engines. But when America entered the war, the Packard Motorcar Co. took a large part of the responsibility for mass-producing Merlins, with the result that a shortage never materialized.

While the Halifax and the Stirling combined with the Lancaster to create Britain's strategic bombing force, the ability of the Lancaster to carry a greater load and defend itself more effectively made it the true star of RAF Bomber Command, and the airplane best remembered as the decades passed.

The most spectacular use of the Lancaster involved dropping spinning bombs developed by Dr Barnes Wallis to destroy several major German hydroelectric dams and turn vast areas downstream from them into lakes. They flew into heavily defended areas at near-zero altitude, held their courses while absorbing terrible punishment, and made history, though barely half of the airplanes made it back.

As the war in Europe was ending, plans were put into action to make Lancasters suitable for the final mass assault on the Japanese home islands. This included what would have been the first operational use of in-flight refueling, had the war not ended just a few months after V-E Day.

In the final accounting, the range, capacity and survivability marked the Lancaster as probably the finest all-round heavy bomber of the war.

Mk.X

RAF KB889 – Imperial War Museum, Duxford,
RCAF KB944 – Canadian Warplane Heritage Museum
RAF PA474 – Battle of Britain Memorial Flight

Avro Lincoln

The demand for improved speed, defensive power and durability of bombers was so great during World War Two that it was said, for example, that no two B-17s rolled out of the Boeing factories in exactly the same configuration. But there has to be a limit to the extent of the changes an airplane can absorb before it becomes necessary to start on a new design from scratch. That was the case with the Lincoln.

Specifications of Mk.X

Length: 68ft 11in
Wingspan: 102ft 0in
Height: 19ft 6in
Wing area: 1,297 sq ft
Empty weight: 41,000lb
Maximum speed: 270mph at 19,000ft
Range: 2,230 miles at 210mph, with 7,000lb of bombs
Service ceiling: 21,500ft
Maximum bomb load: 14,400lb

Some Surviving Examples

Mk.I
RAF R5868 – RAF Museum, Hendon

Its predecessor, the Lancaster, retained the same general outlines for all of its career, as many of the minor and even major changes were interior. But the need for a new heavy bomber had become obvious while the Lancaster was still at the peak of its production. While the Lincoln looked very much like its younger sibling, at least from a distance, it had 18 feet greater wingspan, higher aspect ratio, more than 100 sq ft of additional wing area and more powerful Rolls Royce Merlin engines. This combination produced significant improvements in speed, range and service ceiling.

The purpose of the shift to a newer airplane was directly related to its proposed use in a major expansion of the bombing attacks on Japan prior to the planned invasion of German-occupied western Europe. When the prototype Lincoln flew shortly after the D-Day invasion of France, this was a perfectly reasonable expectation.

The first Lincoln was received by 57 Squadron at East Kirkby in 1945, and was being prepared for operations in the Far East, but its fate (as well as that of Japan) had already been sealed by hundreds of B-29 Superfortresses that exceeded its performance in all respects, and were already in action against the Japanese. The final act was the atomic bombing of two Japanese cities and the end of the war.

The production of most Lincolns – more than 500 – occurred after the war's end, with the airplanes remaining in RAF service until 1963, after years of use in the Far East.

The successor to the Lincoln was the Shackleton, a long-range maritime patrol bomber that was clearly a relative of the Lancaster, but was powered by four Rolls Royce Griffon V-12s driving contra-rotating propellers. It was armed with 20mm cannon in three low-drag turrets, and first flew in 1949. The next bomber to carry the Avro name was the Vulcan, a delta-winged craft propelled by four large turbojet engines and bearing not the slightest visual or technical similarity to any of its ancestors.

Specifications

Length: 78ft 3in
Wingspan: 120ft 0in
Height: 17ft 3in
Wing area: 1,421 sq ft
Loaded weight: 75,000lb
Maximum speed: 319mph
Range: 1,470 miles
Service ceiling: 30,500ft
Maximum bomb load: 14,400lb

Surviving Example

B.2
RF398 – Royal Air Force Museum, Cosford

Short Stirling

The four-engined, long-range heavy bomber was a major element in the Allies' war plans against the Axis powers, though Germany, Italy and Japan failed to see the strategic impact of this particular weapon as something worth stressing. While the value of the unloading of millions of high-explosive and incendiary bombs on enemy targets can never be precisely quantified, few question the impact, despite the tens of thousands of pilots, radio operators, navigators and gunners who lost their lives while delivering the bombs.

America built B-17 Flying Fortresses and B-24 Liberators at the same time, in case one of the types turned out to be significantly superior, or one failed to live up to expectations. In Britain, three heavy bombers were developed together, and while the Lancaster and Halifax became major offensive weapons, the Short Stirling was soon revealed to be clearly inferior, thus justifying the multiple-type plan.

The official requirement at which the Stirling was aimed was one of the most challenging ever. The new four-engined bomber had to be able to carry 14,000lb of bombs for 2,000 miles and cruise at 230mph at an altitude of 15,000ft while sporting three drag-producing gun turrets. Moreover, it had to be designed for quick conversion into a troop transport, and even had to be easily dismantled for carriage by train! If this wasn't already too much,

the experts behind their sturdy oak desks wanted the bomber to be able to take off in 500ft after clearing a 50ft barrier!

Shorts applied much of their experience gained during years of designing and building large flying boats to the new airplane, hoping to use the wing and much of the fuselage that were already flying as the Sunderland patrol bomber. When the RAF insisted it reduce the wingspan to 100ft as their rivals were doing, the result was a thicker, lower aspect ratio wing which had considerably greater drag and thus reduced performance from the original design. When the German anti-aircraft system became a major headache, the inability of the Stirling to climb above its range proved yet another handicap.

The Stirling might have lost out to an airplane from Supermarine, but when a German air raid destroyed the prototypes of the latter, the RAF had little choice but to go with the Shorts airplane. The first prototype of the Stirling crashed when its landing gear failed after the first flight, and the second didn't fly until the autumn of 1939. Enemy raids interfered with production to the extent that only 15 had been delivered by September, 1940. Nevertheless, the Stirling had become the first four-engined heavy bomber to see action, in the previous August.

Combat operations increased gradually, as the initially slow production rate picked up speed. As the US 8th Air Force was not ready to assume its role as the daylight bomber force, the RAF handled this as well as night raids. Thanks to effective defensive armament and surprisingly good maneuverability, Stirlings were initially able to fight off many of the German defenders, until the fighters learned its weak points and began attacking in greater numbers.

By the end of 1941, 150 Stirlings had been delivered to squadrons, but by then the German fighters and anti-aircraft gunners were taking an increasing toll, and so the bombers were diverted to night raids. While the airplane was the recipient of a steady stream of improvements, its performance never approached that of the Lancaster or Halifax, and so its usefulness as a heavy bomber rapidly decreased by September, 1944.

From then on, they were relegated to jobs as a transport, glider tug and mine-layer. The final production version – the Mk.IV – was built as a dedicated transport. When production ended, 2,375 had been built, far fewer than the Halifax or Lancaster, but still enough to have a significant impact on the war in Europe, despite their poor start.

No direct descendant appeared and the next Shorts project was the Belfast turboprop transport in 1966.

Specifications

Length: 87ft 3in
Wingspan: 99ft 1in
Height: 22ft 9in
Wing area: 1,460 sq ft
Empty weight: 44,000lb
Maximum speed: 270mph
Range: 2,000 miles with 3,500lb of bombs
Service ceiling: 17,000ft
Maximum bomb load: 14,000lb

Surviving Example

Mk.III

ML824 – Royal Air Force Museum, Hendon (as recovered from crash site)

Bristol Blenheim/Bolingbroke

In the mid-1930s military aviation was characterized by open cockpits, fixed landing gears, miles of struts and wires and acres of fabric covering. Truly, the airplanes were just advanced versions of those that fought in World War One. But another big war was on the horizon and it was time to modernize with new materials and new shapes and much more powerful engines.

In Great Britain, the Royal Air Force was still demonstrating to adoring crowds at its annual exhibitions at Hendon its majestic-but-awkward twin-engined Overstrand and Bombay bombers, along with sprightly little Gladiator and Fury fighters. Not everyone was as complacent as many of those at the top of the military services. The Bristol Aeroplane Co., for example, in 1936 rolled out its slick and sleek Type 135, which was neither bomber nor fighter but instead was promoted (at least publicly) as a small airliner or even as what later became known as an executive transport.

With a pair of new 350hp sleeve-valve engines, it would cruise near 180mph, as fast as any British bomber of the day, thanks to thin stressed aluminum skin, retractable landing gear, three-bladed metal propellers and nary an external strut nor wire. One of the first interested customers was happy with everything about the 135 but its limited range, and so the Type 142 was more to his liking, with 640hp Bristol Mercury radial engines and an estimated top speed of 250mph. Here was a civilian airplane that was as fast as the RAF's top fighter, the Gloster Gladiator!

Government tests soon showed an actual top speed of 285mph at *full loaded weight*, a figure that did not escape the notice of the Royal Air Force and quite possibly the Luftwaffe, as well. This was 30mph faster than the RAF's newest fighter, which was but a little closer to production. What was to become the Blenheim first came to international attention when the civil prototype was displayed

at the 1934 Paris *Salon International de l'Aeronautique*, where it attracted considerable attention as just about the most modern airplane in the show.

The process of developing the civil 'Britain First' into the Blenheim began in July 1935, long before the Nazis began 'annexing' previously independent neighboring countries. An order was placed for 150 Blenheim Mk.I, with the first of them flying less than a year later.

By the end of 1936, production had reached 24 per month, though changes were made regularly. A fully-equipped Mk.I was much heavier than the early versions, yet would still reach 285mph at 15,000ft. More than 1,500 of this version were built by Bristol, Avro and Rootes and they began to enter service with the RAF in March 1937. That same year, a Mk.I was converted into the prototype for the Mk.IV for which the wing was raised from the low position to mid-wing, and the unusually short nose was extended to a more conventional location. These changes resulted in a poorer field of view for the pilot, and so the nose became more glass than metal to compensate.

By the time the war started in September, 1939, most of the Mk.Is had been replaced by the Mk.IV, though some of the first version saw action in the Western Desert. The export version had been built for Finland, Turkey, Yugoslavia and other nations.

A Blenheim was the first airplane flown on an offensive mission in World War Two by any of the Allies, with a single Mk.IV taking off one minute after Britain officially declared war on Germany for a mission to photograph the German fleet at Kiel. The next day, 10 Mk.IVs attacked German warships in the RAF's first bombing mission of the war. They continued to be used until late 1941.

The Blenheim, however, suffered the same fate as other pre-war designs, in that it had too little defensive armament to fight off formations of fighters during daylight missions. Scores were destroyed in action, and others on the ground, until they were withdrawn to night operations. This resulted in one of the Blenheim's major contributions to the development of the effective night fighter, operating with crude-but-effective Airborne Intercept (AI) radar as early as July, 1940.

The last of more than 4,000 Blenheims were retired from bombing operations in mid-1942, when they made way for Douglas Bostons and deHavilland Mosquitoes. Many Mk.IVs were produced in Canada as the Bolingbroke.

Produced in parallel with the Blenheim was the visually similar Beaufort, although larger and more powerful and which served until 1944.

Specifications

Length: 42ft 9in
Wingspan: 56ft 4in
Height: 12ft 10in
Wing area: 469 sq ft
Empty weight: 9,790lb
Maximum speed: 265mph
Range: 1,950 miles
Service ceiling: 31,500ft
Maximum bomb load: 1,300lb

Surviving Examples

Blenheim Mk.IV
RAF BL200 – Finnish Air Museums
RCAF 10201 – (ex-Bolingbroke) Imperial War Museum, Duxford

IV T
10038 – Brussels Air Museum

Bolingbroke Mk.IV
RAF 9892 – Canadian Air & Space Museum, Ottawa
RAF 9893 – Imperial War Museum, Duxford
RAF 'L8756' (10001) – RAF Museum, Hendon

Bristol Beaufort

As far back as 1936, the steadily increasing expectations of another war produced two airplanes aimed at the need for a land-based, twin-engined torpedo bomber. The first, Blackburn's Botha, was so seriously lacking in stability and performance that not even a larger type of engine could bring it up to the speed expected for the original lighter weight version. Unacceptable losses in its brief period of combat resulted in its being relegated to training squadrons, where additional losses brought the realization that it was simply a failure in its basic design.

Its successful rival – the Bristol Beaufort – bore a strong family resemblance to a direct predecessor, the Blenheim, and was seen as a general reconnaissance bomber, as well as a torpedo-carrier. In fact it was intended as a replacement for the Vickers Vildebeest, an early-1930s open-cockpit biplane that could barely exceed 150mph and had a defensive armament of just two hand-held .30 cal. machine guns. As such, it was the RAF's only torpedo bomber in service at the start of the war.

The Beaufort, which was larger, heavier and more powerful than the Blenheim, first flew in October 1938, powered by two Bristol Mercury sleeve-valve engines that initially were exchanged for more powerful Bristol Perseus, which still couldn't enable it

to reach the speed of the older Blenheim. Finally, Bristol Taurus engines were installed in improved cowlings. Other problems arose when the prototype was undergoing tests of its bombing capabilities, but most of these had simpler solutions.

The first Beauforts entered Costal Command squadron service in January 1940, with more than 1,000 Mk.Is following until the 900hp Pratt & Whitney Wasp-powered Mk.II was ready to take its place.

As was becoming a pattern, the early Beauforts lacked the kind of defensive armament needed to stand a chance against German Bf 109s. Four .303-cal machine guns were added: two in the nose and one on either side of the fuselage. Then, when the Taurus engine revealed problems, it was proposed that the Pratt & Whitney Twin Wasp be substituted, but the lack of assurance that they could be supplied in sufficient quantity and in time, forced Bristol to rely on the slightly inferior Taurus.

Only 680 Beauforts were built in England, along with slightly more in Australia. Regardless, the type became a mainstay of the anti-shipping war, particularly in the Mediterranean and the Atlantic, as well as closer to home in the English Channel and North Sea.

They were eventually replaced by Bristol's own Beaufighter, which had proven a superior launching platform for not only bombs and rockets, but torpedoes, as well. The last Beaufort was built in 1943, and the last retired from service a year later.

Specifications of the Mk.I

Length: 44ft 7in
Wingspan: 57ft 10in
Height: 12ft 5in

Wing area: 503 sq ft
Loaded weight: 21,230lb
Maximum speed: 265mph
Range: 1,600lb
Service ceiling: 16,500ft
Maximum bomb load: 1,600lb

Surviving Example

RAF DD931 – RAF Museum Hendon

Handley Page H.P. 52 Hampden

If only World War Two had started a few years earlier, the Hampden might have earned for itself an honored place in the annals of combat aircraft. As it was, by the time the war had begun the Hampden had been flying for three years and as the result of the rapidly accelerating pace of aeronautical technology, was quickly fading into the background.

When the prototype first flew in June 1936, it was on the cutting edge of progress. Unlike the wire-braced Heyford bomber then coming out of the same factory direct to RAF squadrons, it was of all-metal, flush-riveted, stressed skin construction. Power came from a pair of supercharged Bristol Pegasus nine-cylinder, sleeve-valve radial engines turning three-bladed controllable-pitch metal propellers.

All this and an especially clean fuselage and modern airfoil produced an outstanding speed range of 75mph to 265mph. For a twin-engined bomber it had very good maneuverability. The original plan had been to build two versions, the second being powered by 24-cylinder Napier Dagger liquid-cooled engines and

called the Hereford. Serious mechanical problems with the engines resulted in most being re-engined back into Hampdens.

On the negative side were shortcomings common to all British bombers of the day, and were the fault of those laying down the specifications, rather than designers and builders. It had but four .30 cal machine guns, none of which offered much field of fire and whose limitations quickly became known to German fighter pilots.

While better bombers were in the works, Hampdens were available when war came along, and were pressed into actions which severely challenged them. When war began there were eight squadrons of Hampdens, with a formation of them launched on a raid a day later. It quickly became apparent that their lack of defensive armament was a critical failing, and they were soon relegated to night attacks and dropping propaganda leaflets.

When the need arose for airplanes to lay mines in enemy waters, Hampdens were drafted and then sent on night raids, where their ability to withstand battle damage proved of great value. In May 1940 they joined with another obsolete type – the Armstrong Whitworth Whitley – on the first bombing raid on German soil. They also took part in the first raid on Berlin, in August 1940, and the first 1,000-bomber raid in May 1942. They took part in night bombing raids until September 1942 then continued to be used in other operations through December 1943.

Production continued until March 1942, with 1,420 being built in English factories and another 160 in Canada. For an airplane designed in an earlier era, it proved surprisingly adaptable to the rapidly changing demands of a war eventually being waged by propeller-less airplanes and pilotless flying bombs, which could hardly have been imagined when the Hampdens first flew.

Surviving Examples

B. Mk.1

RAF P5436 (with parts from AN136 and N132) – Canadian Museum of Flight

RAF AE436 – RAF East Kirkby, Lincolnshire (long-term restoration)

Hawker Hart and Audax

The Hart was the first of a long series of Hawker fighters and bombers that symbolized the era with their compact, streamlined engine cowlings and minimal struts and wires, though fixed landing gears and open cockpits remained standard. When the prototype Hart flew in 1928, it was a bomber that was as fast and maneuverable as any British fighter, and a major step forward from

Specifications

Length: 53ft 7in
Wingspan: 69ft 2in
Height: 14ft 11in
Wing area: 668 sq ft
Loaded weight: 18,750lb
Maximum speed: 250mph
Range: 2,000 miles
Service ceiling: 22,700ft
Maximum bomb load: 4,000lb

its predecessors that bore strong similarities to the airplanes of the latter part of World War One.

Since 1927, the RAF's main light day bomber had been the Hawker Horsley, which had bested such rivals for a contract as those paragons of anonymity, the Handley Page Handcross and the Bristol Berkeley. Horsleys served until 1935, even though the first of some 460 Harts had joined squadrons as early as 1930.

The Hart's outstanding features were its speed and versatility, which apparently more than compensated for its limited bomb load which, at 500lb, was inferior to the Horsley, which could carry either 600lb of bombs or a single 2,150lb torpedo. The Hart was powered by a 525hp Rolls-Royce Kestrel V-12 and was armed with two .303-cal. machine guns. Though a bomber, it could easily out-run the Armstrong Whitworth Siskin, the RAF's main fighter when the Hart was introduced, and the Bristol Bulldog which was the main fighter of the mid-1930s.

So adaptable was the Hart that more of them were built as two-seat Hart Trainers than as bombers. Among the bomber versions were the type C for communications, the Hart India and the Hart Special, a tropical version which had desert equipment including a new radiator with large sand filters, as well as brakes on the main wheels.

A modification of the standard Hart was powered by a 530hp Rolls Royce Kestrel X engine and called the Audax. Used for Army co-operation functions, it differed from the Hart in having a long, out-slung exhaust pipe and an under-fuselage hook for picking up messages from the ground in those days of crude, unreliable radios. More than 600 were built, with a few still in service with the RAF in Africa early in the war, and others serving as late as 1941 as glider tugs.

Other developments of the Hart included the Hardy, a ground-support attack bomber that entered service in 1935, the Hind, which served from 1935 until 1938 when it was replaced by monoplane bombers such as the Fairey Battle and Bristol Blenheim, and the Demon, which was the first two-seat fighter purchased by the RAF since World War One.

Specifications of the Hart

Length: 29ft 4in
Wingspan: 37ft 3in
Height: 10ft 5in
Wing area: 348 sq ft
Loaded weight: 4,555lb
Maximum speed: 185mph
Range: 470 miles
Service ceiling: 21,300ft
Maximum bomb load: 500lb

Surviving Examples

Swedish Air Force 714 – Swedish Air Force Museum
Real Aeroplane Co., Breighton

Specifications of the Audax

Length: 30ft 6in
Wingspan: 37ft 5in
Height: 11ft 6in
Wing area: 349 sq ft
Take-off weight: 4,380lb

Maximum speed: 170mph
Range: 375 miles
Service ceiling: 21,000ft
Maximum bomb load: 550lb

Surviving Example

Historic Aircraft Collection

Hawker Hind

When Britain became convinced that it had to be prepared to deal with a re-arming Germany, the RAF launched a major expansion plan. To outfit a sudden growth in the number of combat squadrons required a great boost in aircraft production. As the high-performance monoplane bombers and fighters were still in the development phase, there was little choice but to fall back on improved versions of the tried-and-true open-cockpit biplanes which had been its mainstays since the beginning of World War One. It wasn't an ideal solution, but anything had to be better than simply waiting.

Hawker's Fury fighter and Hart bomber were obvious choices for minor improvement that would not delay production unnecessarily. The Hart and the Demon, which became the Hind, were equipped with a more powerful Rolls-Royce Kestrel V liquid-cooled V-12, and the Hind would become a standard light bomber until the single-engined Battle monoplane and the twin-engined Blenheim monoplane could be built in sufficient numbers.

The prototype Hind flew in September 1934 with a more efficient Fairey-Reed two-blade metal propeller. It went into service with frontline squadrons in November 1935, with the assumption that they would be pulled out as soon as practicable. With a bomb load barely over 500lb and a range of just over 400 miles, its utility would be severely limited.

By 1937 Hinds were already being replaced, and at the start of the war only a single squadron had them in use, and then only in the army cooperation role. The Hawker replacement was the Hector, still an outdated biplane design although with an 800hp Napier Dagger H-24 engine. Six Hectors were used in a dive bombing mission against German troops on the French coast as late as May 1940 in what was probably the last hurrah for the British biplane bomber.

The Hind by then had been relegated to the trainer function, taking novice pilots who had been flying deHavilland Tiger Moths

in September 1938. While the Hind was well on the way towards obsolescence when it began its service life, it did its job, helping to prepare for the coming war which saw aviation leap from biplanes to turbojets.

Specifications

Length: 29ft 7in
Wingspan: 37ft 3in
Height: 10ft 7in
Wing area: 348 sq ft
Weight: 5,300lb
Maximum speed: 185mph
Range: 430 miles
Service ceiling: 26,400ft
Maximum bomb load: 485lb

Surviving Examples

– RAF Museum, Hendon
– Real Aeroplane Co., Breighton
41.H.8.1899 – RAF Museum,Cosford
41.H.8.1902 – Shuttleworth Collection, Old Warden Aerodrome

into the more rarified atmosphere of high powered flight. While they ceased being used for training in Britain before the war started, Canada and New Zealand continued to find them of use in this function.

As late as 1941 saw Hinds in action on the part of the South African Air Force against the Italians in Kenya, by the Yugoslavs against German and Italian air forces, and by Iran against British and Soviet ground forces invading their country. With only a fixed .303 cal. machine firing forward and another from the rear cockpit, they could hardly have been able to deal with even the earliest versions of the new monoplane fighters.

In barely a hint of the unprecedented numbers of military airplanes to come, 528 Hinds were built before production ceased

Bristol Brigand

It isn't always enough to have a top-flight engineering department and a long tradition of building first-rate light bombers and torpedo bombers. Not even having the full support of the military air arm at which your new machine is aimed. The timing has to be right, even after production has begun. Long-term planning may suddenly change as a result of changes on the part of the enemy. Or it may be a combination of little shifts that add up to one big one.

In the case of Bristol's powerful, heavily armed Brigand, it descended directly from the Beaufighter, through the Beaumont ground-support fighter-bomber that was never built, to the Buckingham with its two 2,500hp Centaurus sleeve valve engines that ended up as the Buckmaster trainer, to a pure torpedo bomber called the Buccaneer, which soon became the Brigand.

The prototypes of the Brigand were ordered in April 1943, when the outcome of the war still looked grim. The first one didn't leave the ground until December 1944, when an Allied victory was becoming increasingly likely and the need for a dedicated land-based torpedo bomber was not. More than that, the basic concept of propeller-driven combat airplanes appeared increasingly out-dated in view of the amazing performance of even the earliest and not always thoroughly tested jets. The enormous effort that had gone into refining internal-combustion engines since their first use more than 40 years before, may have resulted in a mere stepping stone to totally different engines that offered unimagined power and reliability.

The war ended before a single Brigand could venture into combat. That finally happened in 1946 during an uprising in Iraq. Soon, Brigands replaced the Hawker Tempests and Beaufighters, which had joined in action in Malaya.

The use of Brigands in the Far East revealed weaknesses that had not been experienced at home. Normal weather caused rubber seals to fail, and then the long blast tubes used for the 20mm cannon allowed hot gases to accumulate and ignite the high-explosive shells. Yet another mechanical failure – that of a complete propeller blade – was caused by corrosion of a small metal part.

When its dive brakes' leather bellows rotted away, more than one airplane lost a wing in a steep dive. The accumulation of limitations created by these problems led to the Brigands being replaced by deHavilland Hornets, and soon grounded.

Specifications

Length: 46ft 5in
Wingspan: 72ft 4in
Height: 17ft 6in
Wing area: 718 sq ft
Loaded weight: 39,000ft
Maximum speed: 358mph
Range: 1,980 miles
Service ceiling: 26,000ft
Maximum bomb load: 2,000lb

Surviving Example

RH746 – under restoration for the RAF Museum, Hendon

Short Sunderland

World War Two marked the high point of the flying boat era and its swan song. From the day in 1909 when Henri Fabre first flew off water until the war-necessitated widespread use of variable-pitch propellers and long hard-surface runways, the sea had provided the only 'runways' suitable for heavily-loaded aircraft to take off and land.

The dream of trans-oceanic airline and airmail service began to take form in the early 1930s, with the American Sikorsky

and Boeing flying boats, and those of Britain's Short Brothers & Harland. While the Sikorskys took the lead in long-range service, this soon motivated Britain to seek its own four-engined transports to carry air mail to far-flung outposts of the British Empire.

A contract for 28 new-style flying boats was awarded to Shorts for 28 examples of the S.23. At about the same time a specification was announced for a large flying boat to be used for long-range reconnaissance. Shorts offered a version of its S.23, as the S.25, while Saunders-Roe designed its S.33, both of which were ordered in prototype form.

The first Shorts S.22 flew in October 1937 and a modification of it was powered by four 1,000hp Bristol Pegasus engines. It was the first to carry the name Sunderland. Its huge hull had space for, among other things, two decks with a galley, a fancy flush toilet and even a limited machine shop for in-flight maintenance. For an aircraft intended to fly for many hours without landing, these seemed to be necessities rather than frills as might first have been viewed.

Construction was state-of-the art, with metal, flush-riveted skin. Defensive armament included a rare-for-the-day power-operated tail turret with four .30 cal. machine guns, and sufficient fuel for missions of as long as 14 hours, though at quite low cruising speed. Additional guns were added as reports from the field revealed their need.

While planned for anti-submarine use, Sunderlands went into action upon the start of the war, rescuing crews from sunk merchant ships wherever they were needed, from British coastal waters to the Mediterranean Sea. They were among the first types to employ radar against surface vessels, and while the first attempts were foiled by German counter-measures, these were made ineffective by the more advanced radar carried by the Mk.III.

Though the Sunderland's guns were of the relatively small .30 cal., enough were installed to make the life of an attacking German airplane unpleasant. On one occasion, a Sunderland was set upon by eight Ju 88s, shooting down three and doing enough damage to the others during an extended battle that the attack was broken off and the flying boat was able to stagger home.

While the intensive use of flying boats ended with the cession of hostilities, the RAF kept some in service and they were used in the Berlin Airlift, the Korean Conflict and other, less famous actions until 1959. A few were operated by the French Navy until 1960, and the Royal New Zealand Air Force as recently as 1967.

Of the 750 Sunderlands built, a few remained in use as the civil Hythe, and an improved version known as the Sandringham was briefly operated as an airliner in the late 1940s.

Specifications of the Sunderland Mk.III

Length: 85ft 4in
Wingspan: 112ft 10in
Height: 32ft 11in
Wing area: 1,487 sq ft
Loaded weight: 58,000lb
Maximum speed: 210mph
Range: 1,780 miles
Service ceiling: 17,600ft
Maximum bomb load: 5,000lb

Surviving Examples

Mk.III

c/n SH-57C – Musee de l'Air, le Bourget
RAF ML814 – Fantasy of Flight

Mk.IV

RAF NJ203 – Oakland (California) Aviation museum (ex-Howard Hughes)

Mk.MR.V

RAF ML796 – Imperial War Museum, Duxford,
RAF ML824 – RAF Museum, Hendon

Fairey Swordfish

It looked more like a left-over from a World War One movie than anything that could possibly be of use in the far more technological World War Two. A biplane, it retained the open cockpit, fixed landing gear, clutter of struts and wires, and fabric covering that epitomized flying machines of that bygone era. Yet it flew quite effectively with the Royal Navy all through the 1939–1945 War.

The Swordfish had its immediate origins in a requirement issued in 1930, with the prototype flying in February, 1934, at which time it was very much in line with contemporary thinking. It was intended to be a two-seat, carrier-based torpedo bomber with the additional function of fleet reconnaissance, designed and built for the Greek Navy. The major difference from what became a well-known design was the use of a 525hp liquid-cooled Rolls Royce Kestrel V-12 engine turning a two-bladed metal Fairey-Reed propeller.

It was tested with, first, the standard two-wheel landing gear as well as a single main float plus two smaller wingtip floats for balance on the water. Another airplane, developed in parallel by Fairey, used a 625hp Armstrong Siddeler Panther 14-cylinder radial engine, the style generally preferred for naval airplanes due to their greater resistance to catastrophic combat damage. It had ailerons on all four wing panels and connected by what later became known as slave struts.

The version that eventually was placed in production had a slightly longer fuselage and a mild rearward sweep of the wings to return the center of gravity to where it had been with the shorter fuselage. This did not interfere with the Swordfish's ability to have its wings folded for convenient storage in the limited space below a carrier's flight deck.

It was a combination of unusually good maneuverability and very low minimum speed that made it useful in low-level operations, where enemy fighters were at a disadvantage due to the proximity of the sea. In fact, it is claimed that a greater tonnage of enemy shipping was destroyed by Swordfishes than any other type of Allied aircraft.

The biplane, which was clearly obsolete before the war began, equipped the first Royal Navy squadrons as early as the summer of 1936, while no fewer than 13 squadrons of them were operated by Fleet Air Arm squadrons at the war's start, and the number would eventually hit 25. Fairey's more modern Albacore was intended to replace the Swordfish, but development was slow, and so what was being affectionately called the 'Stringbag' proceeded to make history.

In April, 1940, a single Swordfish, operating as a spotter plane for the Royal Navy in the waters off Norway, enabled a sole British warship to send seven German destroyers to the bottom. At the same time, another Swordfish dive-bombed a U-boat in a near-by fjord, causing it, too, to sink.

By November, 1940, they launched the Battle of Taranto aimed at keeping the Italian Navy from helping its Axis partner. Three Italian battleships and a cruiser were heavily damaged by torpedo attacks, which put them out of commission. Of the 20 Swordfish sent into the battle, only two were lost. The following May saw these outdated biplanes do the critical damage to the greatly feared German battleship *Bismarck*, after which surface ships were able to methodically pound it to ruins.

As late as September, 1944, they were still proving to be a thorn in the Germans' side by providing aerial escort to vital supply convoys on the northern route to Russia. Soon, however, they were relegated to anti-submarine duties, where their newly-installed radar and unguided air-to-surface rockets proved of great value. The final operational unit was not disbanded until a few days after the end of the war in Europe.

A total of almost 2,400 Swordfish was built before they were replaced by Fairey's Barracuda, a much more modern torpedo bomber that never approached the stature of its predecessor in the hearts of its pilots.

Specifications

Length: 36ft 4in
Wingspan: 45ft 6in
Height: 12ft 10in
Wing area: 607 sq ft
Loaded weight: 4,190lb
Maximum speed: 140mph
Range: 545 miles
Service ceiling: 10,700ft
Maximum bomb load: 1,600lb

Surviving examples

Mk.II
FAA P4139 – Fleet Air Arm Museum
RN NF370 – Imperial War Museum, Duxford
RN HS469 – Shearwater (Canada) Aviation Museum

Fairey Albacore

The Albacore was a more powerful, more streamlined and more comfortable Swordfish, and clearly intended to replace the venerable torpedo bomber. But it was so much less maneuverable that its predecessor not only remained in service during the Albacore's time, but continued well after the latter had been replaced by more modern airplanes.

The Swordfish, beloved by its crews, nevertheless had its share of shortcomings. It was drafty to the point of being frigid in the bitter weather of northern areas in which it often operated. In an effort to correct this problem, the Albacore was heated, though the rear of the cockpit remained immune to efforts to keep out the cold winds. It could also become uncomfortably hot in the summer.

When the first prototype of the Albacore didn't fly until late 1938, Swordfishes had been delivered to active squadrons some two and a half years earlier, which should have given Fairey ample opportunity to absorb combat experience into their newer design. A major source of the delay was the Bristol Taurus engine, which was replaced by a later version. The first Albacores were not received by a Fleet Air Arm unit until March 1940, by which time the Swordfish had been established as a dependable part of the force.

At first, Albecores were operated strictly as land-based airplanes for mine laying and convoy escorting. They didn't begin to fly missions off carriers until November, when they escorted a convoy all the way to South Africa. The following March saw their appearance in a major naval battle, when they damaged an Italian battleship with torpedoes despite heavy anti-aircraft fire.

What followed were several actions in which they imparted limited damage to enemy ships but took major losses. Many Albacores were soon returned to Britain to again operate from land bases, and by 1942 they were starting to be replaced by much more modern Barracuda monoplanes having considerably better performance. They continued to perform escort duties with convoys to and from ports in northern Russia, flying off carriers.

Specifications

Length: 39ft 10in
Wingspan: 50ft 0in
Height: 15ft 3in
Wing area: 623 sq ft
Loaded weight: 10,600lb
Maximum speed: 160mph
Range: 930 miles
Service ceiling: 20,700ft
Maximum bomb load: 1,600lb

Surviving Example

Mk.I
FAA N4389 – Fleet Air Arm Museum

Fairey Battle

For an airplane that was ordered in the summer of 1935, it was a major step forward. In an era of biplanes, it was a monoplane. In an era of airplanes with fixed landing gears, its was retractable. In an era of airplanes whose airframes were covered with fabric, it used aluminum. And it was the first to be powered by the ultimately legendary Rolls Royce Merlin V-12.

Nevertheless, the Battle was a failure in combat and soon was relegated to the status of a trainer and a test-bed for experimental radical-design engines. It may have suggested the shape of bombers and fighters to come, but simply lacked the performance. By all rights its name should probably have been transferred to a more potent aerial weapon.

Britain's Air Ministry and the engineers at Fairey should be given considerable credit for their foresight, as the airplane that was ordered in 1934 and rolled out for its engine-delayed first flight in March 1936 must have looked to many as almost futuristic. When it turned in a top speed of 240mph, as against a promised 195mph, the future should have looked bright.

While it was certainly faster than any other British bomber, realistically it should be compared with friendly and unfriendly fighters, as its success in combat would depend on its ability to fend fighters off. By the time the first Battle flew, the Messerschmitt Bf 109 was well into its test program, having already displayed a top speed of 290mph and due to receive a more powerful engine at any moment.

On the home front the Battle would be completely outclassed by the 320mph Hurricane and 350mph Spitfire. On the basis of speed alone, the Battle was obsolescent almost as soon as it left the ground.

Manning a Battle were three men: a pilot, a radio operator/gunner who sat at the back of the long canopy, and a bomb-aimer/

observer who lay prone on the bottom of the fuselage, behind the pilot. The defensive armament consisted of just two .303 cal. machine guns, one fixed in the right wing and the other hand-operated and pointed aft. This would prove to be entirely insufficient to deal with the pilots of nimble Messerschmitts who soon found its many weak spots.

Any bomber relies on its range and load of bombs to do its job, and there the Battle also came up short. The early ones could carry but 1,000lb of bombs for less than 1,000 miles, and so would have to be assigned to anti-shipping use in the waters immediately surrounding the British Isles, and to attacks on the French coast, once fighting reached that stage.

The Battle began its combat life with a flourish, being the main bomber type flown to France the day after the war began, and being the primary type making up the Advanced Air Striking Force. As this was the beginning of the 'Phoney War', they were used for reconnaissance operations, though one of them earned the honor of being the first RAF aircraft to shoot down a German airplane, a Bf 109.

The inability of a Battle crew to defend itself soon became obvious, however. When an all-out effort using all the remaining airplanes was launched on troops and bridges in and around Sedan, France, most of the 63 attackers were shot down. All those that could still fly were promptly sent back to England, where they took part in minor night raids on the occupied coast. The final combat operation was in October, 1940.

Of the 2,200 Battles built, more than half were shipped to Canada and Australia to be used mainly as target tugs and trainers. Their usefulness had not ended, as they were then used to flight-test experimental engines including the 24-cylinder Fairey P.24 Prince, a variety of Rolls Royce Merlins, the Napier Sabre and Dagger, the Bristol Hercules and Taurus, as well as a variety of propellers.

Specifications

Length: 52ft 1in
Wingspan: 54ft 0in
Height: 15ft 6in
Wing area: 422 sq ft
Loaded weight: 10,800lb
Maximum speed: 240mph
Range: 1,050 miles
Service ceiling: 23,500ft
Maximum bomb load: 1,100lb

Surviving Examples

Mk.I
RAF L.5343 – RAF Museum, Hendon
National Military Museum, Brussels

Chapter 3

Union of Soviet Socialist Republics

Ilyushin Il-2 Stormovik

It was as classically Russian as a military airplane could be, aimed at overwhelming the enemy with numbers. It was too heavy and underpowered to lift a large load of weapons so its commanders counted on masses of them attacking together. More Stormoviks were built than any other type of combat airplane (as many as 36,000), but more than half of them were shot down by German fighters and anti-aircraft gunners. Still, there was what seemed like an unending supply of pilots and airplanes in the pipeline, ready to take their place.

The Il-2 may have been the most heavily armored of single-engined bombers, as its fuselage was partly composed of a thick, 10,000lb armored shell around the crew, engine, radiators and fuel tanks. This cut the useful load to a few air-to-ground rockets that still might have wreaked havoc, had not their load of explosives been reduced to a level far below that of the rockets fired by other anti-tank airplanes such as the Hawker Typhoon and the Republic Thunderbolt.

The prototype of the Il-2 flew in October, 1939, and revealed one of the many weaknesses of the system which had been shredding its own officer corps because of imaginary plots to oust those in power. The engine for this low-altitude ground-support airplane was designed to produce its maximum power at *high* altitude.

A second prototype, with a more appropriate engine, didn't fly until October 1940, and by June 1941, as Germany, despite its non-aggression pact with the USSR, attacked its 'ally' along a broad front, only 25 had been built.

The demand for tank busters in the face of thousands of German tanks was so great that no industrial organization could have satisfied the need. Moreover, the manufacturing facilities were exceptionally crude, and the masses of workers poorly qualified for their jobs. The thousands of mechanics needed in the field to keep the airplanes operating around-the-clock were not much better prepared. But not-exactly subtle threats from Josef Stalin, plus the knowledge that he would do anything to get his way, proved to be a successful motivation to those who built Il-2s, those who flew then and those who repaired them.

Late in the war, the Il-2 began to be replaced by Ilyushin's Il-10 Stormovik, a more powerful and more maneuverable version which remained in production long after the end of the war.

And when you build several tens of thousands of any one type of airplane, enough of them can be thrown into action to make a major difference, even if they are being shot down by the scores and hundreds. It's a bit like swatting flies: no matter how many of the annoying little things you kill, there will always be more of them.

Specifications

Length: 38ft 6in
Wingspan: 47ft 11in
Height: 11ft 2in
Wing area: 414 sq ft
Loaded weight: 14,020lb
Maximum speed: 250mph
Maximum Range: 475 miles
Service ceiling: 19,700ft
Maximum bomb load: 1,325lb

Surviving Examples

Il-2 (composite) – US National Air & Space Museum
Il-2m3 – Pima Air & Space Museum

Ilyushin Il-10 Stormovik

No matter how good an airplane may be, there is always room for improvement, assuming that there is time and there is demand. When the proposed improvements are sufficiently extensive, the result may be a new airplane, rather than a series of modifications to the original. This was the case when the Il-2 was replaced by the Il-10, even if they looked like two versions of the same airplane.

It was during the epic Battle of Stalingrad – late 1942 into early 1943 – that what became the Il-10 began to take shape. At first, both Ilyushin and Sukhoi offered designs built around the M-71 radial engine, which never got into production. Next it somehow became the Il-1, a heavily-armored interceptor, which, because of its weight, would not have been able to catch, let alone destroy, newer enemy bombers which were about to come on line.

Finally, the Il-1 was converted into a two-seat ground-support airplane, in the same class as the earlier Il-2. Production wasn't started until August 1944 of the original version which carried a fixed forward-firing armament of two 23 mm cannon and two .30-cal. machine guns, with a .50-cal. machine gun for the backseat gunner. Power was from a single 1,800hp liquid-cooled Mikulin V-12 engine.

The offensive load consisted of many combinations of bombs of various sizes and types which added up to a maximum of 1,300lb. Additionally, an Il-10 could carry several unguided air-to-ground rockets, and sometimes even grenades which could be ejected from the aft fuselage and would descend by parachute.

The first airplanes entered service in early 1945, taking part in the final push of Soviet forces to Berlin and beyond. When the USSR entered the Pacific war against Japan, a few days before the dropping of first of two nuclear bombs and the final surrender of Japanese forces, Il-10s were flown in missions from Korea against ships and trains.

Production (especially as the Avia B.33 on license by Czechoslovakia) and operation of the Il-10 continued by North Korea against United Nations forces, and later by the People's Republic of China in minor skirmishes against the Republic of China (Taiwan). The last of 4,600 built were not retired until 1972.

Specifications

Length: 36ft 9in
Wingspan: 43ft 11.5in
Height: 11ft 6in
Wing area: 323 sq ft
Loaded weight: 14,410lb
Maximum speed: 310mph
Range: 620 miles
Service ceiling: 24,610ft
Maximum bomb load: 1,300lb

Surviving Example

B.33 (license-built in Poland)
Polish Air & Space Museum, Kracow

Ilyushin DB-3

It was the Red Air Force's first modern, monoplane, long-range medium bomber, its earliest predecessor having flown as far back as 1935. By the time it got into action, it was becoming obsolete, and was being replaced by hundreds of B-25 Mitchells, thanks to Lend-Lease. The B-25 offered far greater speed and as much as four or five times the DB-3's defensive firepower.

Ilyushin's BB-2, which had failed its tests for a contract, became a long-range bomber test-bed (for the TsKB-26) that flew in 1935 on the power of two license-built Gnome-Rhone Mistral radial engines. It had a wooden fuselage despite the growing trend toward all-metal airplanes, but was not only highly maneuverable but set several world class speed and altitude records.

It was followed by the true prototype of the DB-3, which entered production in the summer of 1936. Manufacturing required special skills and a degree of precision not previously experienced by the Ilyushin workforce, and this slowed progress noticeably. The first test flight by a pre-production airplane came in May 1937, and displayed impressive performance well above that required by the terms of the contract. Top speed was 240mph and its range 1,000 miles with 1,700lb of bombs, considerably better than the Heinkel He 111 which was then generally seen as the new standard for light bombers.

In 1938–1940, more powerful Russian-built engines with variable-pitch propellers led to the final M-87B engine, which boosted the high-altitude performance. But the critical issue of defensive armament received no improvements, remaining at just three .30-cal machine guns, one of which was in the upper fuselage position and one in the lower, and somehow were expected to be operated by the same gunner.

A few weeks after the Germans ignored their 'friendship pact' with the USSR and invaded on a wide front, a small formation of DB-3s made history by dropping bombs on Berlin. The actual baptism of fire by the Ilyushin bomber pre-dated that by two years, when airplanes supplied to the Chinese repeatedly bombed cities held by Japanese invaders. In 1940 they were in action in the first war against Finland.

Production, which totaled just over 1,500 airplanes, ended in 1940.

Specifications

Length: 47ft 8in
Wingspan: 70ft 4in
Height: 14ft 9in
Wing area: 706 sq ft
Take-off weight: 16,890lb
Maximum speed: 267mph
Range: 2,360 miles
Service ceiling: 31,800ft
Maximum bomb load: 4,400lb

Surviving Example

Russian Air Force Museum, Monino

Tupolev SB-2

The SB-2 (originally called the ANT-40) first entered into combat during the Spanish Civil War, which served very effectively as a rehearsal for World War Two. It achieved its peak performance

after its designer, Andrei Tupolev, recognized as one of Russia's greats, had been imprisoned on trumped-up charges during a widespread purge of 'enemies of the state' by dictator Josef Stalin.

It was the first Soviet bomber to be covered with aluminum alloy stressed skin, replacing the corrugated aluminum which is best known for its use in the Junkers Ju 52 and Ford Tri-Motor. The need for high speed even by bombers was becoming accepted in all major air forces, though their development was not always able to keep pace with theory.

A general requirement for a high-speed bomber was issued in 1933, when air forces were still flying clumsy biplanes with forests of struts and wires. Tupolev proposed two versions, one powered by Wright Cyclone radial engines and the other by Hispano-Suiza V-12s, as no domestic engine offered sufficient power for its weight. Both prototypes flew in 1934 and showed themselves to be superior airplanes.

The Hispano-engined version was the second to fly, yet despite extensive developmental problems, went into production with the license-built engines. Many from the first production run found themselves in Spain, where they impressed both sides with their performance. Licensed production was planned for Czechoslovakia in 1938, but not a single airplane had been built by the time the Germans occupied and annexed that country.

Regular improvements were made as the result of combat experience in Spain, though the common problem of insufficient defensive armament persisted. The two hand-operated, nose-mounted .30 cal. machine guns had a limited field of fire and were of almost no use against head-on attacks. The installations of the single hand-aimed machine guns on the top and bottom of the aft fuselage were improved, but still were not up to the rapidly rising standards.

Even before World War Two had begun, the SB-2 was becoming out of date, though the switch to the license-built Hispano engine helped, as did the tight cowling which replaced one that made it look like a radial engine was inside. But even in Spain, where SB-2s were able to out-run the opposing Fiat CR.32s and Heinkel He.51s, the appearance of early-model Messerschmitt Bf 109s changed the game.

When Stalin had so many of his top airplane designers thrown into prison camps, one of them became effectively a relocated design bureau where very talented men continued creating airplanes, though by candlelight. At this point, Tupolev was replaced by his second-in-command, Alexander Arkhangelsky, who proceeded to improve the SB-2 into what became the Ar-2, with improved streamlining, more power and more guns.

Production began in 1940 and continued despite the presence of the far superior Pe-2 which arrived to replace it. In all, almost 7,000 SB-2s were built until the assembly lines were shut down in 1941. They carried the load of bombing operations well into the German invasion, surviving as night bombers at the end.

Specifications

Length: 40ft 3in
Wingspan: 66ft 8.5in
Height: 10ft 8in
Wing area: 560 sq ft
Loaded weight: 12,635lb
Maximum speed: 255mph
Range: 745 miles
Service ceiling: 31,200ft

Surviving Example

Russian Air Force Museum, Monino

Petlyakov Pe-2

Long before the prototype flew, the Pe-2 was embroiled in drama and controversy. The lead designer, Vladimir Petlyakov, replaced Andrei Tupolev, who had been jailed on highly questionable

The design team was then given all of six weeks to convert a high-altitude escort fighter into a ground-attack airplane. Major changes included the removal of pressurization and supercharging, and the addition of dive brakes, bomb bays in the fuselage and engine nacelles and a position in the nose for the bombardier. Against all odds, the rework was completed.

Under the life-or-death pressure directly from dictator Stalin, the prototype Pe-2 flew just before the end of 1940. A year later, the Pe-2 had become one of the stars of the Red Air Force, with performance rivalling that of the de Havilland Mosquito. But the Pe-2 also had some serious shortcomings, including the tendency of its non-self-sealing fuel tanks to burst into flames as a result of machine gun fire, and the usual lack of effective defensive armament in the face of rapidly improving fighter performance.

It wasn't until the latter part of 1941, when the Soviet Air Force was putting itself back together after the first major German winter offensive, that the Pe-2 became a highly effective dive bomber that was fast enough to prove a challenge to the Bf 109s while becoming ever more useful as a bomber. Losses were at first completely unacceptable, becoming less so when modifications to the airplane's fuel system and arrangement of machine guns solved most of its problems.

The Finnish Air Force operated Pe-2s, though hardly in the numbers that the USSR did. During the 1941 Continuation War, the Finns received Pe-2s from their temporary allies, the Germans, from among those captured from the Russians. The use of the airplane for dive bombing led to engine problems, so they were switched to photo-reconnaissance with the result that the Finns were able to stop any Russian advance thanks to prior knowledge of their positions. Often, the Finnish Pe-2s were escorted by Luftwaffe Bf 109s.

charges. Soon, Petlyakov followed, accused either of selling the plans to what became the Pe-2 to the Nazis, or delaying design work on Tupolev's ANT-42 high-altitude escort fighter. Petlyakov was then ordered to lead a group of imprisoned engineers to design the VI-100, which was the ANT-42 after its designer's 'disgraced' name had been removed.

The VI-100 turned out to be a very advanced airplane, with a pressurized cockpit, elaborate electrical system and an all-metal airframe. Its first flight in December 1939 and inclusion in the annual May Day parade revealed outstanding performance, and led to the engineering team being released from prison. Just before mass production was set to begin, the Red Air Force decided that the effectiveness of low- and medium-altitude ground support operations would be more productive, and the VI-100 was cancelled.

Total production of the Pe-2 was 11,400, many of which continued in service long after the war's end, with the Czech, Polish and Yugoslav Air Forces flying them well into the 1950s.

Specifications

Length: 41ft 6.5in
Wingspan: 56ft 3.5in
Height: 13ft 1.5in
Wing area: 490 sq ft
Loaded weight: 18,735lb
Maximum speed: 335mph
Range: 930 miles
Service ceiling: 28, 900ft
Maximum bomb load: 2,200lb

Surviving Example

Russian Air Force Museum

Petlyakov Pe-8

It was intended from the mid-1930s to replace the already-obsolescent TB-3, and was the only Soviet four-engined heavy bomber to be built during World War Two, and certainly the only one with an open cockpit to see any action. The Pe-8 had all the other current modern improvements: smooth stressed-skin construction, supercharged engines, retractable landing gear and three-bladed metal constant-speed propellers (copied from a Hamilton-Standard unit). While the design was promising, the USSR's inability to supply it with an engine that combined the needed range, speed and capacity with reasonable reliability delayed production for several years.

The prototype, which flew in late 1936, had a single large supercharger serving the four Mikulin AM-34 engines, and which was powered by a piston engine buried in the fuselage, but the complicated system was soon dropped. Armament consisted of a single 20mm cannon in the top and tail turrets, two .30 cal. machine guns in the nose turret and one .50 cal. machine gun in the rear of the two inner engine nacelles. All but the tail gun were hand operated.

The flight of the second prototype was delayed considerably by the arrest of chief designer Vladimir Petlyakov during the purge of thousands of alleged subversives. Adding to the production problems were the shortages of high-quality materials for this advanced design, and the lack of skilled workmen. As a result, the first production order was delayed until 1939.

As if the big bomber was jinxed, the first completed airframes sat without engines, as their production had been cancelled. Two new engines were tried, one of them a diesel, but neither met the airplane's needs. Finally, officials settled on the AM-35A. But by then, the factory was being taxed to its limit to provide the excellent Pe-2 light bomber to the Red Air Force. At last, a satisfactory radial engine was developed, but its installation required numerous changes in the defensive armament.

The first long-range mission for the Pe-8 was to Berlin in July 1941, and was as much for morale-boosting as enemy-destroying. Of eight which took off, only two returned, while the commander's airplane was attacked by his own fighters. Most of the losses were blamed on engine problems. By the end of August, 12 more were gone, and the remainder had their engines replaced by AM-35As, which ran more reliably but reduced the range. On missions

Wing area: 2,031 sq ft
Loaded weight: 73,470lb
Maximum speed: 270mph
Range: 3,385 miles
Service ceiling: 22,965ft
Maximum bomb load: 11,600lb

Surviving Example

Russian Air Force Museum, Monino

through the following May, 14 more were lost, leaving just 17 in service, as replacements were strained to keep up with losses.

Fewer than 100 Pe-8s were built, and so the type never reached the status of a reliable long-range heavy bomber, which the Soviets clearly needed. But with politics playing at least as large a role in decisions as technical matters, even a less severe loss rate would have relegated this type of airplane to a position far down the list of effective weapons.

Specifications

Length: 73ft 9in
Wingspan: 131ft 0in
Height: 20ft 0in

Tupolev Tu-2S

It is difficult enough designing and building a combat airplane with extensive use of advanced technology during wartime. The pressures to get things done too quickly can be enormous. When that must be done with the chief designer in prison, and the manufacturing plant run by men chosen as much for their political reliability as their technical competence, long and unnecessary delays are the least of the concerns.

That was the environment in which one of the USSR's finest military airplanes was designed and built. Andrei Tupolev was arrested in 1936, charged and convicted of being an 'enemy of the state' despite having made greater contributions to his country than any of those who stood in judgment of him. Not until 1943 was he released from a series of prisons which included the infamous Lubyanka, and promptly awarded a Stalin Prize, which can only be seen as a transparent apology.

Despite the appalling working conditions in the 'design office', Tupolev and his team managed to design an unusually modern high-speed daylight bomber intended to match or even exceed

the performance of Germany's Junkers Ju-88. Construction of a prototype was authorized in March 1940, with a first flight the following January producing a top speed of 395mph, which was faster than most of the world's fighters.

Any hope that it would immediately go into production was dampened by the cancellation of the AM-37 engine planned for it, and the replacement by the ASh-82. Then in October 1943, production was ended at a main plant so that it could concentrate on Yak-7 fighters. While the USSR was struggling to emerge from the ways of a technologically backward country, it had to face the limitations of a serious lack of men capable of managing large industries.

It wasn't until early 1943 that the very first production model Tu-2 had been completed, and then another year-plus was wasted by the closing of yet another plant and by bureaucratic interference after the design was ready for service. Finally, in the spring of 1944, large numbers of Tu-2s made their way to front-line airfields.

Once in action, the airplane began to show its exceptional performance. Continued improvements to its aerodynamics kept it faster than any Soviet fighters and quite capable of defending itself in battles with the best of the German propeller-driven fighters.

But throughout its history, the Tu-2 was in the shadow of the Petlyakov Pe-2. Even though the Tupolev had clearly superior performance, the leaders of the Red Air Force appeared to be enamored of the Pe-2 and were able to not only keep it in production after the Tu-2 had proven its superiority, but kept the former's production rate at a far higher level.

Only some 1,100 Tu-2s were built during the war, though it remained in production until 1948, when production ceased after 2,500 to 3,000 (sources differ) had been delivered.

Had the management of its production been on a par with the airplane's performance, the Tu-2 would almost certainly have had a much greater impact on the fighting on the Eastern Front.

Specifications

Length: 45ft 3in
Wingspan: 61ft 10.5in
Height: 13ft 11in
Wing area: 525 sq ft
Take-off weight: 28,220lb
Maximum speed: 340mph
Range: 1,245 miles
Service ceiling: 31,200ft

Surviving Examples

Chinese composite – War Eagles Museum, Santa Teresa, New
   Mexico;
– Polish Air Museum
– Russian Air Force Museum

Tupolev TB-3

The USSR in 1926 was still extricating itself from the ruins created by the 1918 Bolshevik Revolution. To most of the world, it was a backward country, with large sections still mired in the 19th Century. Its air force was composed of airplanes bought or copied from other countries, and its airplane industry was considered incapable of meeting current needs on its own.

The first sign that this might not the case came with the start of planning in 1926 for the ANT-6, which eventually became the TB-3, which was one of the world's first purpose-designed four-engined bombers. While the prototype did not fly until late 1930, it was still ahead in both its thinking and execution of any offensive airplane flown in any other country.

In all fairness, more than a little credit for inspiring this monster airplane must go to Igor Sikorsky, a Russian who built the world's first four-engined airplane – the Ilya Mouromets – more than 80 of which served the Imperial Russian Air Force during World War One as the first strategic bomber. Soon, however, the Communists took over the country and Sikorsky fled to America, where he continued to design large airplanes, mainly flying boats.

The TB-3 consisted of a basic structure of steel beams, covered with thin corrugated metal, with the cantilever (internally-braced) wing stretching 130 feet. Power came from four 600hp Curtiss V-1570 Conqueror engines, which were soon replaced by 720hp BMW V-12s turning two-bladed wooden propellers. The first flight was a near-disaster when power for the open-cockpit, ski-equipped airplane was unexpectedly reduced due to extreme vibration which closed the throttles.

The first production airplanes flew in 1932 and proved to be considerably heavier than the prototype, due to the increased thickness of materials, and to a thick coat of camouflage paint.

they provided particularly good target practice for German fighter pilots and anti-aircraft gunners.

Even while their vulnerability remained high and Germany introduced ever more effective fighters, TB-3s continued to be used during some of the most critical battles, including the defense of Moscow and the ultimately pivotal Battle of Stalingrad. As newer airplanes took their place, TB-3s were converted into paratroop and cargo carriers, with some still in service on V-E Day in May, 1945. The TB-3 was eventually replaced by the Petlyakov Pe-8.

Specifications of main version

Length: 82ft 9in
Wingspan: 137ft 2in
Height: approx. 18ft
Wing area: 2,475 sq ft
Empty weight: 24,200lb
Maximum speed: 122mph
Range: 600 to 800 miles
Service ceiling: 16,800ft
Maximum load: 4,400lb

Surviving Example

Russian Air force Museum, Monino

Bonuses offered to workers for weight-saving suggestions paid off handsomely. To test the value of streamlining the corrugated skin, one airplane was covered with fabric and showed only a slight increase in top speed, but a major increase in its ceiling.

Despite its considerable power, the TB-3 had a low speed due to its fixed landing gear and un-streamlined gun positions. But it could carry a heavy load of bombs and, while it was supposed to have been retired in 1939, was available when Germany invaded in June 1941. The Red Air Force had more than 500 in service, and the Navy 25 more. They were at first used as night bombers, but as the needs changed, were switched to daylight bombing, in which

Chapter 4

Germany

Heinkel He 111

What turned out to be possibly the best medium bomber in service at the start of World War Two, began its life as an airliner which never carried a paying passenger. It saw its first action when several He 111s conducted clandestine pre-war, photo-reconnaissance operations over Russia, France and Great Britain, which were advertised as route-proving flights for Deutsche Lufthansa, the German airline.

The origins of this unusually clean and fast bomber can be found in Heinkel's He 70, a high-speed mailplane that set numerous speed records, though its impact was limited, as so few of them were built. While the He 70 was single-engined, its influence on the twin-engined He 111 was clear, as both had very slim, fully flush-riveted fuselages and wings having a very efficient elliptical shape, at least in the early test versions and early production airplanes.

As the building of combat airplanes was forbidden by the Treaty of Versailles, Germany was busily evading the main provisions of the treaty by building combat and training military airplanes in the USSR. By the time the He-111 came along, however, Germany had become more open in its defiance of international law. Its insistence that the He-111 was a small, fast airliner fooled few.

In fact, it was a poor design for carrying passengers, and moreover bore some of the obvious hallmarks of a bomber, including a transparent nose which suggested it might someday contain a bombardier rather than, say, a stewardess. The first He-111 'airliner' flew in 1936 and in that version was shown to the public in January 1937

Regardless of its ultimate purpose, it was fast and maneuverable and was said to be a pleasure to fly.

Like so many bombers of the pre-war era, it had little in the way of defensive armament. In the Heinkel's case it had three .30 cal. machine guns, one operated through a hole in the top of the fuselage. Twenty-two hundred pounds of bombs were carried in what was called the 'smoking compartment' of the civil airplane.

The He 111's baptism of fire came in the Spanish Civil War in 1937, when they served alongside the forces of Spanish dictator Francisco Franco. Unlike previous versions which were powered by Daimler Benz 601 engines, the H-models in Spain had Jumo 211s, as the DB601s were needed for the steadily increasing production of Messerschmitt Bf 109s and Bf 110s. But they started out with the few defensive guns, which were reasonably effective against the limited performance of the Soviet-built fighters.

This rehearsal for the world war to come paid dividends, in that the Heinkels could be flown in actual, rather than merely simulated, combat. But it also produced the false impression that a few machine guns could fight off any opposition. This distorted view of reality was encouraged by the success of the *Blitzkrieg*

offensive that laid waste to Poland a few years later, also against meager opposition.

When World War Two began with the German invasion of Poland, the Luftwaffe had 1,000 He 111s – and the rate of manufacture was increasing rapidly. It wasn't until the Battle of Britain in 1940 that the weakness of the type was revealed when they faced the RAF's much faster and more heavily armed Hurricanes and Spitfires. Those that weren't shot down were methodically replaced by the much better Junkers Ju 88.

With daylight bombing of heavily defended cities proving disastrous, more emphasis was placed on using He 111s against Allied shipping – with attacks with bombs and the laying of mines – though the lack of sufficient armor made them susceptible to the anti-aircraft guns on many ships. Many were then converted into torpedo bombers, with considerably greater success, especially against convoys carrying supplies to northern Russian ports.

The end of the He 111 appeared near in 1942, when production began to run down as replacements were expected. But the Heinkel He 177 (with four engines stuffed into only two engine nacelles) and the Ju 188 failed to meet expectations and were set aside. The He 111 regained its position as factories turned them out by the hundreds even though they were clearly obsolete.

Steady improvement in power, guns and electronics made the He 111 effective against what many considered the second-rate fighters of the Soviet Air Force, as the Eastern Front assumed an increasingly important role for Germany. As the military situation grew more and more desperate, the use of now-obsolete He 111s became easier to justify despite the escalating losses.

Specifications

Length: 54ft 6in
Wingspan: 74ft 2in
Height: 13ft 9in
Wing area: 943 sq ft
Loaded weight: 23,370lb
Maximum speed: 267mph
Range: 1,740 miles
Service ceiling: 22,950ft
Maximum bomb load: 2,200lb

Surviving Examples

He 111E
.2-82 – Quatros Vientos, near Madrid, Spain

He 111H-20
Luftwaffe 701152, NT+5L – RAF Museum, Hendon

He 111P-1
Luftwaffe 5J+CN – Norwegian Air Force Museum, Gardermoen

One of the last uses of the He 111 came in 1944, when it became a surprisingly effective aerial launching platform for the V-1 flying bomb, especially after an increasing number of fixed launch sites had been captured by the Allied armies.

The most unusual version of this highly adaptable airplane was the He 111Z, a strange contraption composed of two He 111 fuselages joined together with an additional fifth engine on the central portion of the wing. It had the power to tow heavy gliders aloft, but just a few were built despite proposals to develop the airplane into a long-range bomber carrying several Henschel Hs.293 radio-controlled glide bombs, and for long-range reconnaissance.

Junkers Ju 86

The Ju 86 was designed well before the war in parallel with the He 111 as both an illegal medium bomber and a legitimate high-speed airliner, though unlike the Heinkel, a few actually served with Swissair and Lufthansa. The two were quite similar, having state-of-the-art stressed-skin construction, closed canopies and

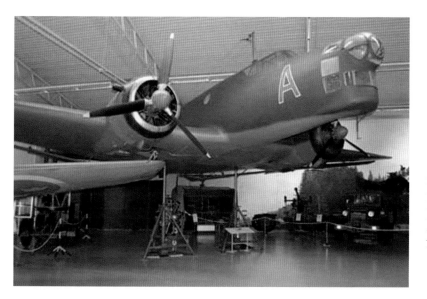

could intercept it. Special British designs aimed at downing the high-flying Junkers came to naught.

Pleased with this new-found use for an obsolete airplane, the Luftwaffe had several dozen earlier Ju 86s modified and used them for missions over Great Britain and the USSR until specially modified Spitfire Mk.Vs shot down several at altitudes as high as 52,000ft, and the Germans soon withdrew them.

The Ju 86 enjoyed good foreign sales, with air forces in Hungary, Portugal, and several South American countries flying them, and Sweden building them under license with BMW engines. A few of the latter remained in service into the late 1950s. The South African Air Force flew them on coastal patrol against German shipping, and then joined RAF bomber squadrons in East Africa until eventually they were retired when more modern Lockheed Venturas became available.

Of 100+ built, the only one to survive is a Swedish-built example.

Specifications

Length: 58ft 7.5in
Wingspan: 73ft 10in
Height: 16ft 8in
Wing area: 883 sq ft
Loaded weight: 18,080lb
Maximum speed: 225mph
Range: 870 miles
Service ceiling: 24,610ft
Maximum bomb load: 1,760lb

Surviving Example

Luftwaffe 860412/Swedish Air Force 115 – Swedish Air Force Museum

retractable landing gear. The Junkers was scheduled to use Jumo diesel engines, but as they were not yet cleared for flight, the prototype was powered by Siemens radial engines, flying with them first in January 1935.

Like the He 111, it was sent to Spain for realistic tests in the Spanish Civil War, where it proved markedly inferior to the He 111, and the few that remained after a short period of action were sold to the Spanish. Ju 86s were tried in the opening days of World War Two during the invasion of Poland, but soon were relegated to less risky operations.

In early 1940, a highly modified Ju 86P was tested with longer wings, a pressurized cabin and special Jumo supercharged diesel engines meant for high-altitude photo-reconnaissance operations. It could fly as high as 39,000ft where no standard Allied fighter

Junkers Ju 87 Stuka

Some aircraft achieve immortality by their beauty of line, others by their outstanding performance, and still others through having simply been at the right place at the right time. In the case of Junkers' Ju 87, it could hardly have been the first, as it was one of history's truly ugly airplanes. Its performance, likewise, was not the sort to impress connoisseurs of speed, maneuverability and efficiency. And so it must be the last, for it was initially thrown into action against pitiful resistance and so appeared to be a far better airplane than would later be revealed.

While dive bombing was not a new idea in the 1930s, its entry into the military's repertoire as a significant element can be traced to a demonstration by US Navy Curtiss Hawk biplanes at the Cleveland Air Races. Among the observers was German World War One ace Ernst Udet, who was also on the program stunting a little Flamingo. The precision 'attacks' on a simulated military target impressed Udet sufficiently that he arranged for the purchase of two of the Hawks by his government and then personally promoted the idea. In late 1941, disgusted with the increasingly irrational behavior of his former friends high in the Nazi Party, Udet committed suicide.

Germany's first dive bomber – the Henschel Hs 123 – flew in April 1935, its development greatly slowed by the need to keep its construction secret from the Allied officials keeping watch on such matters. Before the end of the year, the Rolls Royce Kestrel V-12-powered prototype Ju 87 was being test-flown, though the

airplane soon crashed due to tail flutter. So convinced of the need for dive bombers were many in the Luftwaffe, that construction of additional test models were built, each with a 620hp Junkers Jumo replacing the British engine.

In early 1937, the first Ju 87s produced went to a unit that participated in the swallowing up of Czechoslovakia in the first step in Germany's long-range plan to occupy all of Europe. Soon, several others were sent to Spain as part of the Condor Legion supporting the forces of General Francisco Franco, where they operated with limited resistance to their attacks on key transportation centers. Following the success in that effort, they were used for pin-point bombing of shipping and port facilities.

By the time Germany invaded Poland in 1939, the Stuka was considered a major weapon in Hitler's *Blitzkrieg* plans and was seen as supplanting heavy artillery under certain conditions. In that brief campaign the ability of Stuka pilots to bomb almost at will, due to the lack of effective resistance, played into its propaganda role as the face of modern, unstoppable German warfare. This continued during the invasion of France and the Low Countries, none of which had modern air forces. As long as the Luftwaffe maintained aerial dominance, the dive bombers could operate almost without concern.

It wasn't until Germany launched its pre-invasion assault on Great Britain that the Stuka's fatal limitations became apparent. Despite the Stukas having two .30 cal. machine guns in the wings and a pair firing from the rear cockpit, the RAF's Hurricanes and Spitfires, with their far superior speed, maneuverability and armament, littered the English countryside with pieces of them. Not even the Ju 87D, with its 1,400hp Jumo 211 engine and considerably greater bomb load (up to 4,000lb), could get through the defenses in sufficient numbers to do the sort of damage expected of them.

Quickly redeployed before all of them had been shot down, they were turned into anti-tank weapons for use on the Eastern Front. Despite the Ju 87's obvious shortcomings, a pair of 37mm cannon slung under the wings made it at once a formidable ground-support weapon against the massed tank formations of the Soviet Army.

When production ended in 1944, some 5,700 had been built. But its fame surpassed airplanes that were far superior in all respects and which had been built in far greater numbers. While it achieved its greatest victories against targets that were poorly defended, the image of such an ugly airplane, exaggerated by the frightening screech that accompanied its steep dive at a target like a bird of prey, left an indelible memory on all who had the misfortune to be in its sights.

Specifications of the Ju 87D

Length: 37ft 8.75in
Wingspan: 45ft 3in
Height: 12ft 9in
Wing area: 343 sq ft
Loaded weight: 12,600lb
Maximum speed: 255mph
Range: 620 miles
Service ceiling: 23,950ft
Maximum bomb load: 3,970lb

Surviving Examples

Ju 87B
Luftwaffe 13001643 – Auto and Technik Museum, Sinsheim, Berlin

Ju 87D
Luftwaffe 494083 – RAF Museum, Hendon

Ju 87G
Luftwaffe 494085 – RAF Museum, Hendon

Ju 87R
Luftwaffe 5954, A5+HL – Chicago Museum of Science & Industry
Luftwaffe 5856 – Technishes Museum, Berlin

Junkers Ju 88

It was almost certainly Germany's finest World War Two bomber of any category. In fact, aside from specific functions for bombers (e.g. dive-, torpedo-) there don't seem to have been any clear Luftwaffe distinctions like those common to the Allied air forces. There was no line drawn between light and medium bombers, and since there

wasn't a heavy bomber produced and operated in any quantity by the Luftwaffe, that term loses its meaning.

Design of the original Ju 88 began in January 1936, and the first prototype was rolled out and flown in December of that same year. Its rivals for major production contracts were the Focke Wulf FW 57, which proved to be seriously overweight, and the Messerschmitt Bf 162, which was ruled out because its manufacturer was considered too vital to the building of fighters to stretch its production capacity to bombers, as well.

By the time of the first flight, the Ju 88's chief designer, American Alfred Gassner, had returned home, little being heard from or about him subsequently. Back in Germany, construction of the first of many prototypes proceeded, starting with the Ju 88V-1 in late 1936. It had the simple, clean lines which exemplified the type through a amazing series of versions, including having its Daimler-Benz 900hp V-12 engines inside radial engine cowlings.

Improvements were adopted quickly, the V-3 having 1,000hp Jumo 211 V-12s with direct fuel-injection and two-speed superchargers.

The initially insufficient defensive armament was slowly increased, as was the weight and length of the airplane. The V-5 was cleaned up and somewhat re-shaped for the usual propaganda-related record attempts, and was subsequently flown to an official record of 321mph around a 1,000km closed course with a 4,400lb payload.

Indicative of the enthusiasm of German officials for the Ju 88, plans for the manufacture of complete airframes, or at least major components, included the factories of Dornier, Heinkel, Arado, Henschel and even Volkswagen.

Ten Ju 88As were built for realistic service trials in early 1939. As regular production had yet to build up as scheduled, these test airplanes were sent to an active unit and included in an attack on Scotland a few days after the war had begun.

The late-summer Battle of Britain saw the first major employment of Ju 88s in the conventional bomber role, in which it performed considerably better than the Do 17 and He 111. Manufacture of the type increased rapidly, as did its wingspan, due to steady increases in weight. Speeds dropped, but the tonnage of bombs that could be carried rose. Losses to the RAF's fighters forced the increase in machine guns, including changing to .50 cal., and also the amount and thickness of armor plating protecting the crew.

Some 15,000 Ju 88s were built, most of them as what would be called medium bombers. Others were dive bombers, ground-support/attack bombers with heavy cannon supplementing the usual machine guns, and photo-reconnaissance and special use airplanes. As the He 111s and Do.17s and Do.217s were gradually retired from active roles, their places were taken by versions of the Ju 88, which became the most widely produced non-fighter of the German side of the war.

Despite the constant modifications and experiments to modernize the Ju 88, some proposed changes were too radical, and thus pointed to new designs. The Ju 188 was the first to take shape. The Ju 188 was first produced in 1941 with extended pointed wingtips, 1,700hp BMW801 radial engines and meant for multiple uses including reconnaissance and torpedo bombing, as well as conventional level bombing. The Ju 188S was a high-altitude version with a pressurized cockpit.

About 1,000 Ju 188s were built, and led to the final Ju 388, which had a pair of 1,800hp BMW801 engines for its high-altitude photo-recce operation. Even more advanced versions were proposed but never reached the production stage. The final proposed version was the Ju 488, which was a highly modified Ju 388 with an additional pair of engines.

The most radical use of any of the Ju 88 series and its planned successors was the *Mistel*, in which an unmanned Ju 88 airframe was carried beneath a FW 190 fighter. The lower portion, with its large hollow-charge warhead, was launched at battleships and cruisers, as well as well-defended land targets. About 100 of these were built, and went into action shortly after the D-Day invasion of occupied France. As with so many of the Third Reich's final programs, it was a case of too little and too late to have any major impact on the outcome of the war.

Built in a greater quantity than all other Luftwaffe bombers combined, it was certainly one of the most important bombers of the war.

Specifications of the Ju 88A

Length: 47ft 1.5in
Wingspan: 65ft 10.5in
Height: 15ft 11in
Wing area: 590 sq ft

Normal loaded weight: 26,700ft
Maximum speed: 273mph
Range with Maximum bomb load: 650 miles
Service ceiling: 27,880ft
Maximum bomb load: 4,400lb

Surviving Examples

Ju 88A
Luftwaffe 881478 – Norwegian National Air Museum (as found)

Ju 88C
Luftwaffe 881033 – Norwegian National Air Museum (as found)

Ju 88D
Luftwaffe 430650 – National Museum of the US Air Force
Norwegian National Air Museum

Ju 88G
Luftwaffe 714628 – Deutsches Technikmuseum, Berlin

Ju 88R
Luftwaffe 350043 – Royal Air Force Museum Hendon

Arado Ar.234B-2 Blitz

It was the only jet bomber to see service in World War Two, and then at the end when the few of them that were operational could have little impact on the course of the war. Still, it was a truly historic machine that could have played a much larger (though hardly pivotal) role if it hadn't been for high-level mismanagement.

The basic idea for what would become the Ar.234 was concocted shortly after Germany failed to destroy the RAF during the Battle of Britain. The dream of easily disposing of its major enemy after an unimpeded crossing of the English Channel gave way to a gradual realization that the war would take much longer than the Germans had expected. One of the Luftwaffe's needs was for a fast, long-range reconnaissance airplane.

It was to have a simple high-wing airframe and a pair of Jumo 004 turbojet engines, still under development. The prototype's airframe was completed in late 1941 and was soon joined by several more, and there they sat, waiting for engines to be delivered and installed. The first of the engines finally showed up in March, 1943, after repeated delays as problems with the radical power plant were ironed out.

After extended ground trials, the first flight was achieved in June 1943, though difficulties were still to be experienced with the novel take-off from a droppable three-wheeled trolley, and the use of skids for landing. The near impossibility of post-landing taxying

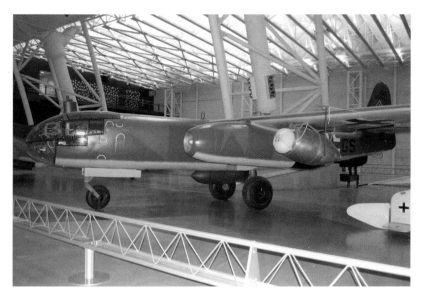

landing as the wheel brakes were not up to the challenge of short runways. They began harassing Allied land forces in France in the latter part of 1944, and then over Italy.

Next came the Ar.234B-2, which was designed to carry a bomb load of as much as 3,300lb, all externally. But it suffered from problems common to the first jets, exacerbated by the need to rush airplanes into combat before they were completely tested and ready. Lateral instability could be pronounced and varied from airplane to airplane. The high aspect ratio ailerons had a tendency to buzz at speeds over 370mph. Restarting a flamed-out engine was possible up to 10,000 feet but not above, and with just a single engine operating, the problems quickly multiplied.

About 150 Ar.234s were completed by the end of 1944, but fewer than half got to operational units due to a long string of difficulties including training accidents, shortage of qualified pilots and other matters which were affecting all of the Luftwaffe as the tide of war turned in the Allies' favor.

Behaving as if the war was expected to last for years, Arado proceeded with tests of a wide variety of versions and even doing what amounted to basic research. The Ar.234C was to be a bomber that could carry a substantially heavier load, while a sub-type was planned to air-launch V-1 buzz-bombs. The C-3 was the fastest yet, with a top speed of 530mph at 20,000ft, while the two-seat C-7 night fighter was to have had four engines, even though its prototype had but two. One prototype was to have used boosting rockets and was built with several sets of wings, two of them swept back and one with a laminar flow airfoil.

When the war ended in May 1944, only 210 of all versions had been built, and fewer than 100 of those had been used in combat. The design's potential had barely been scratched while the rapidly deteriorating organization of the Luftwaffe struggled to combine

had apparently not been considered important. This was eventually solved by the switch to conventional retractable landing gear.

The early prototypes were able to reach 465mph, and it was assumed that with more power, proportionately more speed would be available. Two further prototypes were built with four BMW 003 engines of somewhat fewer pounds of thrust, but the aerodynamics of the airframe limited the speed increase. Regardless, the Ar.234's entry into the war on experimental reconnaissance flights presented the Allies with an airplane that could only be caught after a long dive from much higher altitude. And then only a single pass was possible.

The Ar.234B was the definitive version of the recce airplane, equipped with such modern devices as an ejection seat, a pressurized cabin for high-altitude flying, and a drogue parachute to slow it on insufficiently developed airframes with equally unready engines that were forced to use barely acceptable fuels and be flown by pilots who had the minimum of preparation.

Specifications

Length: 41ft 5.5in
Wingspan: 46ft 3.5in
Height: 14ft 1in
Wing area: 298 sq ft
Maximum Loaded weight: 20,615lb
Maximum speed: 460mph
Range: with 1,100lb bomb load, 965 miles
Service ceiling: 37,700 ft.
Maximum bomb load: 3,300lb

Surviving Examples

Luftwaffe 623167 – National Museum of the US Air Force
Luftwaffe 140312 – US National Air & Space Museum

Fieseler Fi 103/V-1 Buzz Bomb

It was the world's first operational pilotless bomber. It was also the first, crude cruise missile. It was a desperate attempt to frighten the British into… it isn't clear what. But at very little cost, thousands of V-1 'buzz-bombs' were launched at London and other English cities, killing or injuring more than 22,000 civilians. At the same time, the V-1s added to the fears that, with little to lose, Nazi Germany was about to lash out with even more exotic weapons, for which there might be no defense.

It was a bomber with wings and a motor, but no cockpit, no human crew, no instruments, no landing gear, no need for an airfield or repair facilities, let alone a flight training program. Such simplicity may not have been seen in warfare since the days of knights on horseback. But it had its limitations, too. Once launched, it could not be recalled, nor even have its route changed even in maneuvers meant to evade attacking fighters. It flew at a constant 400mph and relatively low altitude: 2,000 to 3,000ft, where it could be challenged by a variety of anti-aircraft weapons, as well as the latest and fastest fighters.

The idea dated back at least to World War One and American Charles Kettering's 'flying torpedo', though none of the early efforts was able to attract sufficient funding and almost certainly lacked the sophisticated technology required for true success. Not until 1936, with Germany dreaming of conquest and of revenge for the punishment it suffered after World War One, did serious work resume on unmanned airplanes or flying bombs.

The Argus engine company, which had flown a remote-controlled surveillance design, backed the work of Fritz Gosslau. In late 1939, a proposal was made to the German Air Ministry for such a machine that would fly 300 miles with a one-ton payload. The remote control unit was seen as the main weakness of the design, and it was rejected. Argus and Arado pressed forward on a modified project, then settled on Fieseler as the chief contractor for what had by then dropped the remote control idea, and redesignated the craft as the Fi 103.

In June 1942, the flying bomb project was approved for what had become a high priority. The first glide test was made from a FW 200 Condor in October, 1942, and the first powered flight was in December, when one was launched from an He 111, as were most of the early test versions.

The first operational flights were made on 13 June 1944, a week after the Allies' D-Day landings on the Normandy Coast of France. What were soon being called the V-1 were launched from easily concealed 'ski-jump' apparatus on the French and Dutch coasts in the pre-set direction of London. Thanks to the raucous throbbing noise and long exhaust flame created by the V-1's pulse-jet engine, the approach could be detected when one was at a considerable distance.

Lacking radio control, the V-1 had to rely on its cleverly simple built-in mechanisms to keep the craft headed in the right direction and at the planned altitude, which made both aerial intercept and the placement of anti-aircraft guns a relatively easy task. An airflow-actuated counter armed the bomb after a few minutes of flight, and after about a half hour, a series of actions sent the V-1 into a steep dive towards whatever happened to be in its way, be it an airplane factory, crowded housing or an open field.

The Germans counted on agents in England to report on the locations of impacts, so that the next batch of V-1s could be adjusted to compensate for errors. The information transmitted from England to Germany was, however, designed to re-route V-1s to unpopulated areas, since all German agents had long since been turned or replaced by the British.

A major effort went into stopping the attacks, including bombing the launch sites and capturing them by ground forces moving through recently occupied countries. As this gathered steam, the Germans switched to more aerial launches from He 111s, though the reduced speed and maneuverability of these already obsolescent airplanes made them easy targets for Allied fighters. The launch of a V-1 at night was easy to spot due to the brilliant light from the engine.

As many as 100 V-1s were launched in a single day towards London, to be met by Hawker Tempests, P-51 Mustangs and the latest Spitfires. Even a few Gloster Meteor jets were thrown into action, the first of their successes being the initial jet-to-jet combat in history. As there were not many critical spots on a V-1 where a few bullets would bring it down, pilots developed the technique of slipping a wingtip under the V-1's wing, rolling and causing the V-1's gyroscopic controls to tumble, which quickly led to a crash.

Of some 10,000 V-1's fired at England, only about 2,400 exploded anywhere near London. But they accounted for more than 6,000 deaths and almost 18,000 injuries, as well as uncountable frayed nerves and hours of lost sleep. The launching of V-1s ended when all the launch sites had been captured, as the lack of precision of the system made it useless for anything but a very large fixed target such as a major city.

The V-1 triggered an interest in unmanned military aircraft that has continued to grow during the succeeding 65 years as the technology has become increasingly sophisticated. The military arms of all the major (and some minor) nations have developed the great-grandchildren of the V-1 into weapons of amazing precision.

Specifications

Length: 27ft 3in
Wingspan: 17ft 6in
Height: 4ft 8in
Loaded weight: 4,750lb
Maximum speed: 400mph
Range: 150 miles
Maximum bomb load: 1,870lb

Some Surviving Examples

Fi 103
Luftwaffe 443268 – Air Zoo Air Museum, Kalmazoo, Michigan
– US National Air & Space Museum
– Imperial War Museum, Duxford,
– Fighter Factory
s/n 2255 – Flying Heritage Collection
– Royal Museum de l'Armee, Brussels
– National Aeronautical Collection of Canada

Chapter 5

Italy

Cant Z.506S Airone

Like so many aircraft hurriedly pressed into service as World War Two loomed, the Cant Z.506 was far from ideal for the purposes envisioned for it. It was, like a lot of civilians who entered the military in those days, in need of substantial changes before being fit for action.

The large, tri-motored floatplane began as a passenger transport and mail plane for the Italian Ala Littoria airline, with seats for only 12 to 14 passengers, despite its size.

The Z.506 was to have initially been powered by three 610hp Piaggio radial engines, while the production 506A had 750hp Alfa Romeo 9-cylinder radial engines. The structure was almost entirely wooden, aside from the 41-foot long metal floats. It entered airline service in 1936, connecting cities along the Mediterranean coast. One of them, flown by Mario Stoppani, set several records in the next two years, including 200mph for a flight of 1,000km at an altitude of 25,000ft with a large payload, and a closed-circuit distance mark of 3,345 miles, all in the appropriate weight class.

The first military version – the Z.506B – was displayed in an aeronautical exposition in 1937 and differed from the civil aircraft mainly in having a long ventral 'gondola' for the bombardier, the bomb bay and a gunner. Armament consisted of a single .50 cal. machine gun in a dorsal turret, and three .30 cal. machine guns – one in the belly and one on in either side of the rear fuselage.

Its first action, as was true for so many Italian aircraft, came during the Spanish Civil War, when it was used for reconnaissance as well as bombing. Almost 100 were being operated by the Italian Air Force, mainly as bombers, by the time of Italy's entry into the war in June 1940. It continued to see action around the Mediterranean, especially during the fighting in Greece. Thirty were ordered by Poland, but only one had been delivered before the Germans invaded in September 1939 and the remainder were kept by the Italians.

It wasn't long before it became obvious that such a large, slow seaplane was at a great disadvantage when opposed by much higher performance British fighters such as the Hawker Hurricane. It was reassigned to reconnaissance units, and then to maritime patrol and air-sea rescue of the victims of ship sinkings and aircraft losses. A few Z.506S were built for the Luftwaffe.

After Italy surrendered to the Allies, 28 Z.506s were operated by Italian units in support of Allied operations, but only on miscellaneous and quite minor functions. Several of the 324 built remained in air-sea rescue service as late as 1959. Like most pre-war civil designs that had been modified for military use, they rapidly became obsolete as their drawbacks limited their usefulness.

Specifications

Length: 63ft 10.5in
Wingspan: 86ft 11in
Height: 24ft 9in
Wing area: 915 sq ft
Loaded weight: 27,115lb
Maximum speed: 225mph
Range: 1,700 miles
Service ceiling: 26,240ft
Maximum bomb load: 2,600lb

Sole Surviving Example

Reggia Aeronautica MM45245 – Italian Air Force Museum

Savoia-Marchetti S.M.79 Sparviero IMAGES 106

Italy's best and most widely used bomber of World War Two was a tri-motor, a layout other countries had long ago replaced with more modern airplanes having either two or four engines. America's B-25 Mitchell medium bomber, considered one of the very best of the war, was of almost identical size, carried the same load of bombs, had the same normal range and had the same top speed, though it did have more power and far more offensive and defensive guns. Yet who thinks of the two airplanes as near-equals?

Like other bombers of its day, it first appeared as an airliner, with a row of passenger windows and now-obvious facilities for guns or bombs. Arriving in 1934, it was as streamlined as anything in its class, but was trapped in an out-dated way of thinking which permitted a wing structure of wood with fabric covering. The fuselage was built from welded steel tube covered with plywood.

Like the Cant Z.506, it was tried with a variety of engines, then settled on three Alfa Romeos which enabled it to break numerous records, a popular pastime with Mussolini's Fascist government, bent on demonstrating Italy's superiority, and not averse to claiming modified production machines were no more than standard production items.

The second prototype was a bomber, with streamlined housings above and below the fuselage for machine guns and gunners, and an area in the center of the fuselage for bombs in place of passengers The nose contained an engine, rather than a bombardier and guns to protect it from head-on attacks, an arrangement that was becoming popular for other countries' air forces.

Along with its standard S.M.79, Savoia-Marchetti developed an export version having but two engines, assuming correctly that other countries would prefer the higher speed and more modern style to the allegedly increased safety of an extra engine.

The S.M.79B had a conventional glassed-in nose with space for a bombardier and a single hand-held .50 cal. machine gun. The upper bulge was gone and the cockpit extended forward for better visibility.

Rumania bought 24 of these which were powered by 1,000hp Gnome Rhone radial engines, then ordered 24 more with 1,200hp Junkers Jumo liquid-cooled V-12 engines. Many more were built in Rumania on license and operated on the Eastern Front.

As far back as 1937, the Reggia Aeronautica experimented with the tri-motor as a torpedo bomber, finding that it was able to launch torpedoes with a greater success than from other airplanes. A version which could carry two full-size torpedoes was put in production and used by both Italy and Germany with considerable success, though the airplane was still at a great disadvantage against Allied fighters.

Despite its out-dated appearance, the S.M.79 was as close to world standards as any Italian warplane. With 1,500 built, it was available for a variety of tasks, most of which it performed well.

Specifications

Length: 53ft 2in
Wingspan: 69ft 6.5in
Height: 13ft 5.5in
Wing area: 657 sq ft
Loaded weight: 24,910lb
Maximum speed: 270mph
Range: 1,245 miles
Service ceiling: 22,965ft
Maximum bomb load: 2,750lb

Surviving Examples

Reggia Aeronautica MM2327 (actual MM 45508) – Italian Air Force
    Museum
Reggia Aeronautica MM24499 – Caproni Museum

Savoia-Marchetti S.M.82PW Marsupiale

Almost every airplane produced during World War Two had
something to recommend it, though in many cases their justification
was expediency more than any sort of superiority. In the case of the
S.M.82, it was almost certainly the best of the wartime tri-motored
designs, most others already becoming recognized as obsolete. It
can thus be considered as the transitional type between tri-motors
whose central engine was of questionable usefulness, and the
much more modern two- or four-engined bombers and transports
coming into widespread use.

The S.M.82 was seen from the start as a combination bomber and
transport, with an upper compartment having seats for 32, and a
lower being set up for cargo. As a bomber, it had little to offer.
As a military transport, it lacked the qualities needed for the role.
It might have made a good civil transport, had there not been a
major war in progress and little demand for anything not geared
to military uses.

The prototype, which was an enlarged version of the S.M.75,
didn't fly until 1939, when all the future combatants had bombers
of considerably greater performance and survivability. As an
admission that the Italian aircraft industry lacked a large radial
engine needed for such an airplane, it was powered by three 860hp
Alfa Romeo 128 engines, which were the Bristol Pegasus built
under license. The nine fuel tanks carried a standard load of some

500 US gallons in tanks that were for some reason considered self-
sealing, but tended to explode when hit by incendiary rounds.

The bomb load was impressive, as up to 8,800lb could be
carried, depending on the need for fuel for long-range missions.
The defensive armament left much to be desired. A single .50
cal. machine gun was mounted in a turret located just aft of the
cockpit, but it lacked reliability and its dispersion of fire was no
greater than comparable weapons in most other bombers. Single
.30 cal. machine guns (built by different manufacturers and thus
a maintenance headache) were mounted in either side and in a
retractable gondola on the underside. This latter weapon was
difficult to use, due to a lack of space for the gunner to move
around.

Even if a S.M.82 could have defended itself, its performance was
far below that needed to pose any great threat. Its realistic cruising
speed of 160mph was slower than that of a Douglas C-47 transport,
let alone every Allied fighter and bomber. It was unable to climb
much higher than 16,000 feet when on a bombing mission, leaving
it a sitting duck for even obsolescent interceptors. The pilots of
modern British Beaufighters and American P-38 Lightnings feasted
on them.

Unlike almost every other military airplane of its day, the S.M.82
used wood extensively in not only its covering but basic structure,
as well. Where there should have been heavy armor plating for
the bombardier, a mere 1mm (barely more than 1/32in) thick steel
sheet protected this vital member of the crew, who also lacked the
comforts of heating, oxygen and pressurization.

Total production was just over 700, most of which came under
German control after Italy surrendered to the Allies in September
1943 and brought many of its airplanes to the Allied side, where
they were received with understandably muted enthusiasm. They

found somewhat greater favor with the Luftwaffe, having slightly better performance than their standard Ju 52s, even if the latter were more durable.

Being readily available, some 30 S.M.82s continued to be flown by the Italian Air Force for 15 years after the end of the war. Even an airplane with so many shortcomings was able to find a niche for itself.

Specifications

Length: 75ft 4in
Wingspan: 97ft 5in
Height: 19ft 8in

Wing area: 1,275 sq ft
Loaded weight: 39,340lb
Maximum speed: 230mph
Range: 1,865 miles
Service ceiling: 19,690ft
Maximum bomb load: 8,800lb

Surviving Example

Reggia Aeronautica MM61850 – Italian Air Force Museum

Chapter 6

Japan

Aichi D3A2 'Val'

The attack on the US air and naval bases in Hawaii in December 1941 by the Imperial Japanese Navy comprised the greatest shock ever experienced by the USA. Convinced that Japan lagged years behind the major industrialized nations in aviation technology, little effort had been expended to keep up to date on developments. The result was the sudden realization that Japan had fighters and bombers that rated with those of any country, and that a crash program was needed to reclaim the lead long thought to be secure.

While the fast, nimble Mitsubishi Zero caused the greatest concern, close behind was the Aichi D3A 'Val' dive bomber which did much of the damage at Pearl Harbor. While they had been in action for more than a year in China, the lack of intelligence information lulled the Americans into thinking that Japan's standard dive bomber remained Aichi's older biplane.

In the face of little opposition, 'Vals', despite their fixed landing gears, dove at will, planting their limited bomb loads on capital ships and major land installations with little concern for the Grumman F4Fs and Curtiss P-40s, most of which had already been put out of action by the first wave of carrier-based bombers and strafing Zeroes.

Following the great success of the 'Vals', especially in the sinking of many of the US Navy's largest ships, the Japanese used them to great advantage in their rapid campaign across the Pacific. This, however, was conducted against older defensive aircraft and produced the incorrect and thus dangerous assumption that the Japanese Naval air arm was unstoppable. In fact, the basic 'Val' was battered by fighters and ceased to be a major offensive element by the middle of 1942. In the May 1942 Battle of Midway, most of a large force of 'Vals' was either shot down by much faster fighters, or ran out of fuel and crashed after their carriers had been sunk.

The design dates back to 1936 and a Japanese Navy requirement for a monoplane dive bomber to replace the biplanes which had been in service for many years. The prototype, which first flew in early 1938, was a disappointment, lacking the promised speed from the 710hp Nakajima radial engine, and having serious directional stability problems. It was followed by a second prototype, with an 840hp Mitsubishi engine and an enlarged vertical tail. The top speed limitation was not considered a serious drawback, as it was low speed that was considered so necessary for a dive bomber to be accurate in its attack. For this reason, the fixed, well-faired landing gear was not modernized.

By the time the first production order for 'Vals' was placed, a larger 1,000hp Mitsubishi engine was available, and the installation of a large dorsal fin actually contributed much to its excellent maneuverability. Armament was fairly standard for this type of

Specifications

Length: 33ft 5.5in
Wingspan: 47ft 2in
Height: 12ft 7.5in
Wing area: 389 sq ft
Loaded weight: 8,050lb
Maximum speed: 240mph
Range: 915 miles
Service ceiling: 30,050ft
Maximum bomb load: 815lb

Surviving Examples

JAF B11-201 – Planes of Fame
– Admiral Nimitz Museum, Fredricksburg, Texas

airplane, with a pair of fixed .30 cal. machine guns in the engine cowl and a single .30 cal. in a flexible mount fired from the rear of the long glassed-in cockpit area.

An even more powerful 1,300hp Kinsei engine came on line in mid-1942, but the appearance of Grumman F6F Hellcats and Vought F4U Corsairs signalled the day of the 'Val' was passing. Those remaining after devastating air battles were withdrawn from the front lines to training units and only reappeared in combat as suicide airplanes, when almost anything capable of flight was thrown into the desperate effort to delay the inevitable Allied victory.

Yokosuka MXY-7 Ohka 11 'Baka'

Flying bombs constituted one of the major innovations of World War Two aviation. Both the Japanese MXY-7 and the German V-1 were shaped like airplanes, having wings, fuselages, engines and tails, but prominently lacked (in the case of the MXY-7) any sort of landing gear, and (in the case of the V-1) a cockpit and its occupant. Both were products of desperation in the final phases of the war, and both pointed the way to a frightening future.

The more bizarre of the two was the Japanese development, as it was intended from the start as a suicide weapon, to be guided to its target by a pilot who knew he was about to die. It appears that the project was not completely thought out, as the Mitsubishi G4M 'Betty' carrier plane had to approach within 20 miles of the target before cutting the flying bomb loose to glide to within sight of the target and then start three small solid-fuel rocket motors. Prior to that point, it was an easy target for fighters accompanying the ships. The bomb's top speed in a dive was near 600mph, but its maneuverability was poor and so while it was difficult to hit with anti-aircraft fire, it was seriously hampered in its ability to strike a moving target, even a ship.

The first use of the MXY-7 came on 21 March 1945, when 16 'Bettys', each carrying one MXY-7, were sent to attack a large American task force which included several aircraft carriers. The 'Bettys' were to have been escorted by 55 Mitsubishi A6M Zeros, but almost half of those failed to reach the target. The over-loaded 'Bettys' were attacked by a force of Grumman F6Fs when 70 miles from the ships, and all abandoned their flying bombs. Only a few of the Zeroes and none of the 'Bettys' made it back, and not one of the ships was hit.

Attempts to use the 'Betty'/MXY-7 combination continued for more than a month, with about 50 (of 850 built) being sent on their missions. Three US Navy ships were sunk and others were damaged before the experiment was called off. The basic idea of suicide airplanes did not end at this point, as hundreds of obsolete airplanes were rapidly converted to the suicide mission, and did extensive damage.

There were grandiose plans to improve on the pioneering MXY-7. The Model 21 – a single prototype built with wings of steel rather than wood. The Model 22 – with a jet engine similar to the experimental Italian CC.2 with a piston engine driving the compressor; 50 were built, but lacked sufficient thrust. The Model 33 – turbojet-powered, to have been launched from a Renzan heavy bomber, which failed to go into production. The Model 43 – turbojet-powered, to be lunched from a submarine, but never

built. The Model 43B – like the 43, but to have been launched by catapult from caves. And finally the Model 53 – a turbojet-powered version to have been towed to the vicinity of its target, also never produced.

While suicide flying bombs appear to have long since ended their very short history, the development of highly sophisticated cruise missiles can be traced back to the success of the unpiloted V-1.

Specifications

Length: 19ft 11in
Wingspan: 16ft 9.5in
Height: 3ft 10in
Wing area: 65 sq ft

Loaded weight: 4,718lb
Maximum diving speed: 575mph
Range: 23 miles
Maximum bomb load: 2,650lb

Surviving Examples

– US National Air & Space Museum
– Fleet Air Arm Museum
– RAF Museum, Hendon
– RAF Museum, Cosford
– National Museum of the US Air Force
– Planes of Fame

Japan 5100 – US Navy Memorial Museum, Washington, DC
Japan 1018 – National Museum of Marine Corps Aviation, Quantico, VA

Aichi B7A2 Ryusei 'Grace'

Most versatile airplanes start out as single-purpose machines and then are 'discovered' or even forced to be adaptable to other functions, On the other hand, the occasional airplane that is designed from the start to be used for more than one purpose rarely succeeds. This was the lot of the otherwise highly impressive Aichi B7A, which was done in by the fates.

The Japanese Navy began World War Two with two distinct offensive airplanes: the Nakajima B6N 'Jill' torpedo bomber and the Yokosuka D4Y 'Judy' dive bomber, both of which served well in their intended roles. But when it came time to replace them with more modern airplanes, it was decided at a high level to create a single airplane which could fulfill both functions. It was a risky move that failed.

The B7A was a large, heavy, powerful machine that was to lift either a 1,650lb torpedo or a pair of 550lb bombs, all to be carried externally where they would reduce the speed at which it could fly. Power was to come from the insufficiently-developed 1,825hp Nakajima Homare 11 two-row radial engine that was to have produced a top speed of 350mph. This would have made it difficult to catch for the Curtiss P-40s and Grumman F4Fs that were in use by the US Army and Navy when the first prototype flew in May 1942.

Had it gone into service after a test program of reasonable length, its unusually heavy fixed forward armament of two 20mm cannon and surprisingly good maneuverability would no doubt have made it a very difficult target in the expected dog fights. But it didn't happen that way. Serious problems with the engine delayed deliveries until late 1944, by which time the nature of the Pacific war had changed.

The Wildcats and Warhawks had been replaced by far faster and more heavily armed Navy Hellcats and Corsairs and by Army Mustangs. Success in air battles was no longer to be expected. Moreover, the need to operate the heavy B7A from large Japanese carriers proved its undoing when almost all the large carriers were sunk in a series of huge sea battles. The B7As were, of necessity, shifted to land bases, where their superior qualities were not so obvious.

This was not the only stroke of bad luck suffered by the program, as the main factory was almost totally destroyed by a huge earthquake in May 1945. As a result, just over 100 were built during the final stage of the war, when the supply of well trained pilots was rapidly being exhausted.

Had the B7A gotten into action in late 1942 as originally projected, it almost certainly would have enabled Japan's aircraft carrier forces to fight on much more even terms with the Allies. But while Japan struggled with major technical problems, its foe was building thousands of increasingly fast, well armed fighters that could sustain heavy combat damage and continue to fight. The B7A was one of many excellent ideas that failed to become reality.

Specifications

Length: 38ft 9in
Wingspan: 47ft 3in
Height: 13ft 5in
Wing area: 381 sq ft

Loaded weight: 8,400lb
Maximum speed: 350mph
Range: 2,050 miles
Service ceiling: 36,900ft
Maximum bomb load: 1,765lb

Surviving Example

USAAF FE-1204 – US National Air & Space Museum

Aichi M6A1 Seiran

The obvious need to attack a distant enemy's homeland during World War Two led to what now seems inescapably obvious: long-range four-engined bombers that can carry heavy loads of bombs

and the defensive armament required for them to survive long flights over unfriendly territory. The Avro Lancaster, Handley Page Halifax, Boeing B-17 and Consolidated B-24 bear witness to both the popularity of this answer and to its effectiveness.

In the case of Japan, however, the proposed solution to the problem could hardly have been more different. The M6A was to have been catapulted off the deck of a very large submarine, which had surfaced within range of the enemy coast! It would then 'streak' toward its target at some 250mph, powered by an Aichi Atsuta V-12, which was a license-built German Daimler-Benz 601. All the while, the backseat gunner would be fighting off squadrons of land-based interceptors with his single .50 cal. machine gun.

The idea dated back to the 1920s but wasn't taken seriously until World War Two when the initial plan had been to build 18 bombers, which would operate from a fleet of I-400 type submarines. Just how a few airplanes carrying less than a ton of bombs, each, could have any detectable impact on the war was far from clear. But work proceeded. The first prototype was completed in October 1943, and flew a month later, with production starting early in 1944, by which time it had been decided to use them to knock out critical parts of the Panama Canal, and thus add weeks to the transit time of American warships from one ocean to the other.

The first production M6As were ready in October 1944, but the earthquake of 7 December 1944 interfered with plans to put the program into operation, as did the increasingly destructive raids by B-29s in the first few months of 1945. Then production of the needed submarines was stopped, as was that of M6As after 20 had been built. The need to defend the Japanese homeland was overtaking all other issues.

Regardless of the rapid deterioration of Japan's fortunes, the program continued almost as if nothing had changed. A special

flotilla was formed, consisting of three I-400 class submarines carrying three M6As each. While considerable testing had been completed, it was proving difficult to launch three M6As in less than 30 minutes, adding to the chances that radar-equipped interceptors could find them on the surface and end the mission.

Plans to attack the Panama Canal were eventually dropped in favor of an attack on a base where American forces were preparing for a mass assault on the Japanese home islands. While the submarine/mini-carriers were sailing toward this new target, word came that Japan had surrendered. The bombers, which were carrying American insignia in violation of international law, were dumped into the ocean.

Only one has survived, after having been surrendered intact by its pilot and eventually donated to the Smithsonian Institution in

1962. It was restored in 2000 and is on display as the only example of a strange project to launch bombers from submarines.

Specifications

Length: 38ft 2in
Wingspan: 40ft 3in
Height: 15ft 0in
Wing area: 291 sq ft
Loaded weight: 7,275lb
Maximum speed: 267mph
Range: 745 miles
Service ceiling: 32,500ft
Maximum bomb load: 1,875lb

Sole Surviving Example

JAF 1600228 – US National Air & Space Museum

Yokosuka P1Y1 Ginga 'Frances'

The combat airplanes used by the Japanese Army and Navy in the early part of World War Two were lightly built, and without armor and self-sealing fuel tanks in an effort to keep their weight down and their maneuverability up. As long as they faced inferior opposition, these compromises paid off. But when the Allies began to re-equip with more powerful and sturdier airplanes that would not catch fire when hit by a few bullets, the Japanese were forced to reconsider their policy.

Change came slowly, and usually too late. New fighters and bombers were heavier and more powerful, hence faster. In most cases they lacked modern fuel tanks and the armor plating needed to protect the pilot and crew and so remained at a serious disadvantage when battling with the latest types being turned out in large numbers by huge factories located far beyond the range of any Japanese bomber.

When it came time to replace the venerable Mitsubishi G4M 'Betty' long-range bomber with something better able to absorb punishment, the Japanese Navy ordered the sleek, powerful P1Y Ginga (Galaxy). Had it been intended for a single purpose such as strategic or tactical bombing, it might have made a name for itself. But those in charge decided it should be a combination level bomber/torpedo bomber/dive bomber. This led inevitably to an airplane that was overly complicated and therefore difficult to produce in quantity by workers with insufficient technical training. In the field, it required a maximum effort to keep one in the air with simple repairs.

Moreover, the engine originally intended – the 1,800hp Nakajima Homare 11 – was neither reliable nor available in sufficient quantities. It was eventually replaced by the more dependable Mitsubishi Kasei 25 of similar power, a move which further delayed deliveries.

Development of what was to become the P1Y bomber dates back to 1940, with the first prototype not flying until August 1943 and not entering squadron service until early 1945. In mid-1944, the first night fighter version – P1Y1-S – flew, with four 20mm cannon mounted atop the fuselage and meant to fire at an angle upward, a technique that was being used by the Luftwaffe. Soon, however, the night fighter revealed its inability to cope with the high-flying Boeing B-29s, large numbers of which appeared far above the Japanese home islands almost every night.

As with other late-war types, the Frances reverted to its original use as a bomber, and then was loaded with explosives for suicide attacks on Allied warships. The plan to produce a modified version to carry MXY-7 rocket-boosted glide bombs was scrapped, as the need to carry the short-range device close to its target area meant that the heavily-loaded bombers would be easy targets for Allied fighters.

As a level bombers and torpedo bombers, the P1Y1 performed well, though they entered combat when there was a serious shortage of well-trained pilots. Total production was about 1,100, with all but about 100 being bombers.

Specifications

Length: 49ft 3in
Wingspan: 66ft 7in
Height: 14ft 11in
Wing area: 592 sq ft
Empty weight: 16,015lb
Maximum speed: 342mph
Range: 2,889 miles
Service ceiling: 30,850ft
Maximum bomb load: 2,200lb

Surviving Example

JNAF 8923 – US National Air & Space Museum

Nakajima B6N2 Tenzan 'Jill'

Nakajima's B5N 'Kate' was nearly out of date by the time World War Two began, but the inability of the Japanese aircraft industry to build a satisfactory replacement kept it in service long enough for it to become one of the most destructive combat airplanes in the Pacific. The inability of Japan to escape from its doomed policy of favoring light weight and high speed over the survivability of an airplane and its crew, meant that both the B5N and Nakajima's subsequent B6N 'Jill' would provide easy pickings for the enemy's anti-aircraft guns and ever more powerful fighters.

While waiting for the B6N to have its many technical problems solved, Japanese Navy pilots in their B5N's spread havoc across the ocean in battles at Pearl Harbor, Midway and the Coral Sea, while taking an increasing beating. A short burst of well-aimed machine gun bullets or cannon shells could turn their airplane into a ball of fire. While the loss of airplanes was serious enough, even more significant were the rapid disappearance of so many of the well trained pilots and large aircraft carriers with which Japan had begun the war.

The requirement which the B6N was aimed at called for an airplane no larger than the B5N, due to the physical limitations of the carriers. Yet it had to be heavier and at least as easy to fly. When the prototype took to the air in early 1941, it displayed a lack of flight stability that would have made it a poor bombing platform. In addition, it suffered from teething problems with its Nakajima Mamoru 11 engine, which was replaced by the slightly better Mitsubishi Kasei 25, as was being done with most other Japanese airplanes of the time.

It wasn't until well into 1943 that the first 'Jills' got into action against an enemy that had used the previous two years in acquiring large numbers of fighters having better handling, more weapons and the wonderfully reliable, 2,000+hp Pratt & Whitney R-2800 radial engine. In the B6N's debut during the Battle of the Philippine Sea, they were shot down so quickly and in such numbers that they had almost no meaningful impact on the outcome. Design improvements intended to modernize the airplane resulted in little increase in performance.

Faced with the growing problem of the shrinking supply of large aircraft carriers, the Japanese Navy transferred most B6Ns to land bases, where their utility was drastically reduced. The last major battle for the 'Jill' was for Okinawa, where many of them were used for kamikaze attacks. The attempt to produce the purpose-built B6N3 for land-based operations amounted to too little and too late, as the war ended before production could begin.

Of a total of almost 1,300 B6Ns built, only one survived combat, suicide missions and non-combat accidents.

Specifications

Length: 36ft 8in
Wingspan: 49ft 11in
Height: 12ft 6in
Wing area: 400 sq ft
Empty weight: 6,635lb
Maximum speed: 298mph
Range: 1,890 miles
Service ceiling: 29,650ft
Maximum bomb load: 1,765lb

Surviving Example

c/n 5350, USAAF FE-1200 – US National Air & Space Museum

Yokosuka D4Y1 Suysei 'Judy'

'If only….' Every nation that has lost a war has spoken these words in whatever language was appropriate. And so it must have been for the Japanese at the end of World War Two. 'If only we had given higher priority to the survivability of our airplanes and crews.' 'If only we had built a fleet of four-engined strategic bombers.' 'If only….'

And perhaps most important of all the achievable goals, 'If only we had insisted on proving each new type of engine before installing them in airplanes and watching them predictably fail.' One after another, potentially valuable airplanes sat idle while over-extended engineers tried to quickly turn experimental engines into reliable sources of much-needed power. Political pressure to push

engines beyond their early limits often led to even more serious problems that could not be dealt with in the field.

As far back as 1938, the Yokosuka Naval Air Technical Arsenal was busy developing a carrier-based dive bomber to replace the Aichi D3A 'Val', which would soon become obsolete even though it would continue to be used with effectiveness for several years. The D4Y 'Judy' was the result, based on the German Heinkel He 118 dive bomber, two examples of which were sold to Japan, which planned to build copies on license. When one of the two broke up during flight tests, the goal was shifted to a new design, still based to a great extent on the Heinkel.

The first prototype of the D4Y1 flew in December 1940, and it wasn't long before a serious problem arose: wing flutter. Convinced that at least part of the cause was the high stresses of dive bombing maneuvers, the Navy switched the D4Y1 to long-range reconnaissance. To reduce the losses to American fighters, the type was switched back to dive bombing after structural changes to the wings eliminated the fear of catastrophic failure from flutter.

Then the need to operate from the larger carriers posed an increasing problem as Japan's fleet of such ships was being methodically eliminated. This was at least temporarily solved by the addition of catapults to bring the smaller carriers into line with international practice. Still, the original engine – the 1,200hp Aichi Atsuta copy of the German Daimler Benz 601 – was replaced with the more dependable Mitsubishi Kinsei 61 radial engine, much preferred by Japanese Navy leaders.

The final version of the 'Judy' was the D4Y4 *kamikaze* fitted with a 1,760lb bomb and three small solid-fuel booster rockets to increase its speed in the final phase of a fatal dive at enemy vessels. It was able to fly as far as 1,500 miles at close to 350mph, thus reducing the chances of interception that had ended the experiment with MXY-7 flying bombs carried into battle under G4M bombers.

More than 2,000 D4Ys were built and contributed as much as any type of Japanese airplane to successful attacks on American and British ships before increased numbers of anti-aircraft guns and faster fighters turned the tide.

Specifications

Length: 33ft 6in
Wingspan: 38ft 9in
Height: 12ft 4in
Wing area: 245 sq ft
Empty weight: 5,820lb
Maximum speed: 357mph
Range: 2,235 miles
Service ceiling: 35,100ft
Maximum bomb load: 1,235lb

Surviving Examples

JNAF 4316 – Yasukuni Jinja Yushukan, Japan
– Planes of Fame

Mitsubishi G4M 'Betty'

Along with the Mitsubishi A6M, the 'Betty' was probably the best known Japanese airplane of the war. Unlike the Zero, the latter failed to live up to its reputation as a modern airplane to be feared. While the Zero had the speed and maneuverability to deal with the Allied fighters in the early part of the war, the G4M paid for its speed and great range with more critical structural weakness and inability to withstand more than a few direct hits from enemy interceptors.

The 'Betty' looked the part of a long-range heavy bomber, and at least on paper it was just that. With unusually long legs and the ability to carry an impressive load of bombs and/or a single full-size torpedo, it could range over much of the western Pacific Ocean, especially important after Japan had captured a series of well-placed islands. As the Japanese aircraft carrier fleet was being wiped out and those strategically located islands re-captured, it became even more vital to the air war, operating from land bases located far from their targets.

As with the RAF and USAAF, long-ranging heavy bombers had become a priority for the Japanese as a worldwide war approached. In Japan, however, the task of developing such an airplane was given to the Imperial Navy, which no doubt would have preferred something amenable to carrier operations. To make matters even more difficult, the new airplane was to be limited to two engines, which would be hard pressed to deliver sufficient power to achieve the combination of range and payload. Something would have to give.

Compromises must be faced in the design of every airplane, but in this case each alternative would produce a substantial reduction in the ability of the G4M to do its job. In line with Japanese policy, the needed weight reduction was achieved to the detriment of the airplane's survivability. A four-engined heavy bomber like those in the works in Britain and the USA, would not have required such a decision, but that had already been ruled out for reasons far from clear.

The need to protect heavy bombers on long-range missions resulted in a version of the G4M to serve as a heavily-armed fighter to accompany the bomber. By the time this had been given up because the 'fighter' turned out to lack the speed of the bomber, a year had slipped by, and the first 'Bettys' didn't see action until the middle of 1941. Used in China against out-dated opposition, they performed well, as had the Luftwaffe's Ju 87s against Poland in 1939. When used to attack ships well beyond the ranger of any defending fighters, they provided proof, if any was still needed, that airplanes are able to defeat even the largest and most heavily armed capital ships, as long as the latter are not well defended.

It wasn't until the G4Ms faced rugged, heavily-armed fighters during the invasions of the Solomon Islands that their shortcomings were revealed as significant. In the first three months after the Japanese attack on Pearl Harbor, three-quarters of the Japanese Navy's total of 240 'Bettys' were gone. Without a replacement ready, production continued, as did the painting of rising sun emblems on the cockpit sides of Allied fighters.

By the time production ended in mid-1945, almost 2,500 had been built, some of them the considerably improved G4M3, but entirely too late to have any impact on the war. The 'Betty's' final mission was to transport high-ranking members of the Japanese government and military to the signing of the formal articles of surrender.

Whoever must take the blame for the overall policy of saving weight of airplanes by ignoring the need for an airplane's self-sealing fuel tanks and armor plating for the crew – be it the General Staff or even Emperor Tojo – set the stage for widespread failure and ultimate defeat. Even the Grumman F4Fs and Curtiss P-40s with which the US Navy and Army entered the Pacific war, while they could not defeat the Zero in classic whirling dog fights, needed only to score a few direct hits in order to set enemy airplanes ablaze. The end of the war could have been forecast when it began.

Specifications

Length: 64ft 4in
Wingspan: 82ft 8in
Height: 20ft 8in

Wing area: 841 sq ft
Empty weight: 17,990lb
Maximum speed: 267mph
Range: 3,725 miles
Service ceiling: 29,350ft
Maximum bomb load: 4,850lb

Surviving Example

– Planes of Fame (derelict)

Nakajima Ki-115 Tsurugi

Desperation does not always bring out the best in men. Sometimes it results in nothing more than embarrassing failure. For Germany's Luftwaffe, it was the plan to build 4,000 Heinkel He 162s a month; for the Imperial Japanese Air Force, it was the even wilder scheme to build 8,000 Nakajima Ki-115s a month. That would have been as many as the entire US aircraft industry at its world-leading peak. The inevitable consequences of failed attempts to defeat an enemy that they should have known could produce far more and far better airplanes to be flown by tens of thousands of properly trained pilots, were hurriedly assembled prototypes that never led to a single airplane in combat.

With the rapidly diminishing supply of purpose-built MXY-7 suicide airplanes that had accomplished little, Japan turned to combat airplanes filled with explosives for last-ditch efforts to wreck Allied plans to invade their homeland. As the supply of these were of finite quantity, the only way out of the impending disaster was to rush into production a quickly designed airplane of minimum complexity that used almost no strategic materials .

While the basic idea of suicide airplanes – piloted bombs – may have been anathema to Western ideas of morality, the scheme showed signs of becoming highly effective. Even if only a low percentage of aircraft launched survived long enough to hit their targets, enough got through the defenses to create havoc. It stood to reason that if enough such devices could be sent into action, they just might discourage the Allies from a massive invasion of the Japanese homeland.

The Ki-115 was structurally simple to the point of being simplistic. Created mainly of wood and steel, it had 'take-off gear' that was intended to drop off after the first-and-final flight had begun, since a landing was not part of the mission. It had simple flight controls and the bare minimum of instruments. It was to have used any engine that could be found, even those dating back to the 1920s!

It sounds like the plan had been concocted by a few Japanese youngsters, and probably would have stood as much chance of success if that had been the case. Not surprisingly, the Ki-115 had poor take-off performance, little pilot visibility, no defensive armament, and flying characteristics rated as far below any reasonable standards. For more than a few to reach their targets would have required a great supply of experienced pilots, few of whom had survived to this point.

Building 8,000 Tsurugis a month would have required vast factories, a huge workforce and a highly organized system to keep the increasingly scarce raw materials flowing. At no time did Japan have such a manufacturing system, and after several years of highly effective bombing by the US Army Air Forces, it is easy to imagine chaos resulting from a serious attempt to build, ready, arm and launch the number of airplanes planned.

As it turned out, the first Ki-115 didn't fly until June of 1945, and total (not daily) production came to just over 100, none of which is known to have been flown in combat. An improved version – the Nakajima Ki-230 – and a version for the Navy were planned, but the sudden end of the war changed everything.

Specifications

Length: 28ft 1in
Wingspan: 28ft 3in
Height: 11ft 10in
Wing area: 133 sq ft
Empty weight: 3,615lb
Maximum speed: 342mph
Range: 746 miles
Maximum bomb load: 1,765lb

Sole Surviving Example

USAAF FE-156 – US National Air & Space Museum

Mitsubishi Ki-21 'Sally'

The Ki-21 was Japan's main heavy bomber into the latter stages of World War Two, even though it would have been classed by the Allies as no more than a medium bomber, and an obsolescent one, at that. It owed its origins to the friendly relations between Japan and Germany in the late 1920s and early 1930s.

Forerunners of the Ki-21 were the Mitsubishi Ki-1 and Ki-20, both of which first flew in 1932 and were German Junkers bombers built on license. The Ki-1 was based on the Junkers S36, built in Sweden, as Germany was still prohibited by the Treaty of Versailles from constructing military airplanes. The prototype was used by Japan during the Manchurian Incident before going into production. The

Ki-20 began life as the G-38 airliner, powered by four diesel V-12 engines and then the world's largest airplane.

Determined to replace these limited-production bombers of foreign design with purely domestic achievements, Japan set out to create its own in 1936. The result of a competition were two quite modern airplanes from a country considered by most outsiders as being limited to buying or borrowing ideas in order to produce copies. Nakajima's Ki-19 and Mitsubishi's Ki-21 were twin-engined, all-metal, cantilever monoplanes that carried their bombs internally and had very similar performance. After flight tests of several prototypes having different engines, the Ki-21 was chosen for production.

The Ki-21 entered service with the Japanese Air Force in the summer of 1938 as a replacement for the Italian Fiat BR.20. The Mitsubishi's baptism of fire occurred over China a few months later, in limited numbers due to slow production. Initial combat action, which was effectively the final stage of development, revealed what would become common shortcomings in easily ignited fuel tanks and limited ability to fight off attacking airplanes.

Both problems were addressed with an improved version of the Ki-21 which had incomplete protection for its fuel tanks, and defensive armament increased to five .30 cal. machine guns, one of which was installed in the tail of the fuselage, to be operated remotely. Yet another improved model had six machine guns and additional fuel capacity.

The final major model was the Ki-21-IIa which had the 1,500hp Mitsubishi Ha.101 engines and became the main Japanese heavy bomber when America entered the war in December 1941. Escorted by Ki-43 'Oscar' fighters, 'Sallys' made their mark in late 1941 and early 1942 as Japan gobbled up much of the southwest Pacific. French Indo-China, northern Australia and all of the Philippines suffered greatly from the lack of effective fighter protection of the Allied forces.

But the situation was about to change, as the early model Custiss P-40 and an increasing supply of Hawker Hurricanes revealed the critical weaknesses of Japan's air forces. One immediate change was the systematic removal of Ki-21s from action and their transfer to support services, many of them being converted into MC-21 civil and military transports, and others used for special Commando-type missions.

Regardless, the 'Sally' remained in production right to the end of the war, in no small part because the production, testing and operations of newer bombers was interrupted by the increasingly effective Allied bombing raids.

Unique among Japanese military airplanes, the Ki-21 was known by three different Allied names. It was first called 'Jane', which was quickly changed to 'Sally' because the former was the name of General Douglas McArthur's wife. Later, some of them were briefly called 'Gwen' after having been mistaken for a completely new airplane.

Specifications

Length: 53ft 6in
Wingspan: 74ft 10in
Height: 14ft 3in
Wing area: 749 sq ft
Empty weight: 10,340lb
Maximum speed: 268mph
Range: 1,680 miles
Service ceiling: 28,200ft
Maximum bomb load: 2,200lb

Surviving Example

– Thai Railroad Museum, Bangkok

Extinct World War Two Bomber Types

USA
Boeing B-15
  'Grandpappy'
Douglas B-19
North American B-21
North American B-28
Consolidated B-32
  Dominator
Lockheed B-37
Vega B-38
General Motors B-39
Vega B-40
Convair B-41
Pratt & Whitney B-44
Vultee A-19
Stearman A-21
Martin A-22 Maryland
North American A-27
Martin A-30 Baltimore
Vultee A-31 Vengeance
Brewster A-32
Douglas A-33
Vultee A-35
Beech A-38 Destroyer
Vultee A-41

Great Britain
Blackburn Botha
Vickers Wellesley
Vickers-Armstrong
  Windsor
Avro Manchester
Bristol Buckingham
Bristol Bombay
Fairey Spearfish
Hawker Henley

France
Amiot 140
Amiot 143
Amiot 350
Bloch MB.150
Bloch MB.200
Bloch MB.210
Bloch MB.310
Farman F.220
Breguet 698
Latecoere 298
LeO.45
LeO.206
LeO H.257
LeO.450
LeO.451
Potez 540
SNCASE. 458

USSR
Ilyushin Il-4
GST 'Catalina'
Sukhoi Su-2

Poland
PZL.23 Karaś

Netherlands
Fokker C.X

Germany
Dornier Do 17
Focke-Wulf FW 191
Henschel Hs 123
Henschel Hs 129
Henschel Hs 130
Henschel Hs 132
Ha 140
Blohm & Voss BV 141
Heinkel He 177 Griffon
Junkers Ju 186
Junkers Ju 188 Avenger
Focke Wulf FW 200
  Condor
Junkers Ju 287
Junkers Ju 288
Dornier Do 215
Dornier Do 217
Messerschmitt Me 264

Italy
Fiat BR.20
Cant Z.1007
Fiat RS.14
Piaggio P.108

Japan
Mitsubishi Ki-30 'Ann'
Kawasaki Ki-32
Kawasaki Ki-48
Nakajima Ki-49
  Donryu/ 'Helen'
Mitsubishi Ki-67 Hiryu/
  'Peggy'
Mitsubishi G3M
Kawasaki 'Lily'